# Why We Disagree about Inequality

# John Iceland, Eric Silver, and Ilana Redstone

———

# WHY WE DISAGREE ABOUT INEQUALITY

## Social Justice vs. Social Order

polity

First published in 2023 by Polity Press

Polity Press
65 Bridge Street
Cambridge CB2 1UR, UK

Polity Press
111 River Street
Hoboken, NJ 07030, USA

ISBN-13: 978-1-5095-5712-7
ISBN-13: 978-1-5095-5713-4(pb)

A catalogue record for this book is available from the British Library.

Library of Congress Control Number: 2022946839

Typeset in 11 on 13pt Sabon
by Cheshire Typesetting Ltd, Cuddington, Cheshire
Printed and bound in Great Britain by CPI Group (UK) Ltd, Croydon

For further information on Polity, visit our website: politybooks.com

# Contents

# 1

# Introduction

The events of May 25, 2020 shifted the US national conversation on Social Justice and Social Order. That was the day George Floyd was killed by Minneapolis police during an arrest after a store clerk alleged that he had passed a counterfeit $20 bill. One of the four police officers called to the scene knelt on Floyd's neck for nearly nine minutes during the arrest, which was recorded by bystanders. Floyd can be heard telling the officers over a dozen times that he can't breathe (Hill et al., 2020).

This shocked and appalled many Americans. It also reignited the Black Lives Matter (BLM) movement. After Floyd's tragic death, protests spread across the United States and the world, sometimes erupting in riots that left at least twenty-four dead in total (Beckett, 2020; Poujoulat, 2020). By the end of the summer, racial inequality had been catapulted to center stage in our national conversation more forcefully than it had in many years.

In the months that followed, different reactions to the protest movement emerged. In a June 2020 *New York Times* opinion piece titled, "America, This Is Your Chance," legal scholar and civil rights lawyer Michelle Alexander hailed the protests as a moment of reckoning. She wrote: "Our only hope for our collective liberation is a politics of deep solidarity rooted in love. In recent days, we've seen what it looks like when people of all races, ethnicities, genders and backgrounds rise up together, standing in solidarity for justice, protesting, marching and singing together, even as SWAT teams and tanks roll in" (Alexander, 2020).

But not everyone viewed these events so positively. Social commentator Heather Mac Donald, in an opinion piece in *City Journal* titled "Breakdown," warned that the rioting was a threat to social order and if left unchecked would culminate in a dramatic spike in violent crime in cities across the country. Mac Donald wrote:

> These are no longer the warning signs of a possible breakdown of civilized life. That breakdown is upon us. If local and national leaders are unable to summon the will to defend our most basic institutions from false and inflammatory charges of racism, they have forfeited their right to govern. Unless new leaders come forth who understand their duty to maintain the rule of law, the country will not pull back from disaster. (Mac Donald, 2020)

Alexander and Mac Donald were reacting to the same events, but their reactions were rooted in competing moral and philosophical perspectives that go well beyond questions of racially biased policing (Silver et al., 2022). Alexander's reaction reflects a Social Justice perspective that is concerned primarily with the plight of the vulnerable. Mac Donald's reaction reflects a Social Order perspective that is concerned primarily with social stability and cohesion.

To further see these two languages in action, consider a second social movement with a far-reaching impact: #MeToo. This movement served the important role of highlighting the problem of sexual assault and

2

harassment, especially in the workplace. The watershed moment of #MeToo was the 2017 exposé of the predatory behavior of Harvey Weinstein, a movie mogul accused by several women of sexual misconduct, including rape. As the allegations against Weinstein surfaced, many women came forward with their own experiences of sexual assault and harassment, thus launching a social movement to reduce gender violence and increase gender equality. While many of the ideals of the movement were widely shared across political divides, the definition of the range of misbehaviors that qualified as "sexual violence" and the preferred methods to address it differed (Silver and Silver, 2021).

In 2017, writer Sophie Gilbert aptly summarized the importance of the movement to so many women, and men:

> The power of #MeToo ... is that it takes something that women had long kept quiet about and transforms it into a movement. Unlike many kinds of social-media activism, it isn't a call to action or the beginning of a campaign, culminating in a series of protests and speeches and events. It's simply an attempt to get people to understand the prevalence of sexual harassment and assault in society. To get women, and men, to raise their hands. Recent revelations about the alleged abuses of Weinstein and Bill Cosby and Jimmy Savile and R. Kelly have proven that truth has power. There's a monumental amount of work to be done in confronting a climate of serial sexual predation – one in which women are belittled and undermined and abused and sometimes pushed out of their industries altogether. (Gilbert, 2017)

However, other commentators argued that, while the #MeToo movement highlighted an important social problem, it also led to excesses. They raised concerns about presumptions of guilt without due process and the flattening of all sexual misconduct into a broad category of sexual violence. As commentator Andrew Sullivan wrote:

> The act of anonymously disseminating serious allegations about people's sex lives as a means to destroy their careers and livelihoods has long gone by a simple name. It's called McCarthyism . . . I'll tell you what's also brave at the moment: to resist this McCarthyism, to admit complexity, to make distinctions between offenses, to mark a clear boundary between people's sexual conduct in a workplace and outside of it, to defend due process, to defend sex itself, and privacy, and to rely on careful reporting to expose professional malfeasance. In this nihilist moment when Bannonites and left-feminists want simply to burn it all down, it's especially vital to keep a fire brigade in good order. (Sullivan, 2018)

The #MeToo movement, like BLM, was inspired by a real social problem, yet it also elicited different reactions. These differing views were in large part reflections of *Social Justice* and *Social Order* concerns. When framed in this manner, we can more easily think through the tradeoffs involved in attempting to understand and solve these and other social problems. For Michelle Alexander and Sophie Gilbert, Social Justice is the salient orienting principle. They are willing to tolerate a degree of social upheaval in order to advance their cause and even view such upheaval as a necessary condition for social change. For Heather Mac Donald and Andrew Sullivan, who see value in the principles of Social Order, these movements have the potential to affect society in alarming ways. In this line of thinking, a too-strong focus on Social Justice in response to highly publicized cases can lead to an overly confident and overly rapid pursuit of social change that, despite good intentions, risks producing unintended negative consequences.

# Introduction

While the divergence between Social Order and Social Justice orientations can prove difficult to navigate even under the best of circumstances, increasing political polarization has made such navigation even more challenging. Because of polarization, elections have become more contentious, with people not only disagreeing with their opponents but often demonizing them. This observation is supported by opinion polls showing that partisan Americans increasingly dislike and distrust members of the opposing party (Iyengar et al., 2019; Molla, 2020).

The central thesis of this book is that two competing moral and philosophical perspectives – one oriented toward *Social Justice* and one oriented toward *Social Order* – constrain our collective conversations about social problems. We argue that the root cause of disagreements over social issues is not party affiliation, but rather a divide in people's moral and philosophical beliefs and intuitions about what constitutes a good and just society and how best to achieve it (Haidt, 2012; Kling, 2017; Marietta and Barker, 2019; Sowell, 2007).

The goal of this book is to describe these two perspectives and put them on equal footing. In doing so, we hope to explain one "side" to the other in order to foster more fruitful conversations and solutions. We believe that complex social problems cannot be addressed without a shared understanding of their causes and magnitude. And to achieve this understanding policymakers and the public must first learn to recognize and become conversant in the moral language of their ideological opponents.

In the pages that follow, we attempt to provide new insight into the nature of a wide range of contemporary public disagreements. In doing so, we hope to help those who hold either a Social Order or Social Justice perspective to recognize the bases of their own convictions and to become better at understanding and communicating with those with whom they disagree – in the hope that we may all get better at working together to formulate effective, data-driven solutions to today's most intractable social problems.

It is unfortunate when efforts to solve social problems founder due to lack of resources, but it is tragic when such efforts founder due to failed communication. We hope this book will help to avoid such tragedies.

## Moral Intuitions, Visions, and Beliefs about Social Order and Social Justice

Psychological research suggests that moral intuitions are strong and relatively stable. They are the result of "fast thinking" cognitions that precede and influence our more deliberate moral reasoning (Greene, 2013; Haidt, 2001, 2012). Psychologist Jonathan Haidt has posited that our moral intuitions coalesce around two broad domains: "Individualizing moral intuitions" encourage us to suppress selfishness for the good of other individuals by putting *the care and protection of individuals* at the center of moral concern. "Binding moral intuitions" encourage us to suppress selfishness for the good of the group by putting *social order and cohesion* at the center of moral concern.

Upon hearing of a woman who feels unsafe when a co-worker tells a joke with sexual content, for example, or a citizen who speaks disrespectfully to a police officer during a traffic stop, many people feel a flash of anger. According to Haidt, those with strong individualizing moral intuitions will react more negatively to hearing about the woman who feels unsafe, while those with strong binding moral intuitions will react more negatively to hearing about the disrespectful citizen. Haidt explains that moral intuitions such as these are present to varying degrees in all humans due to innate mental structures that have arisen in response to adaptive challenges that faced our ancestors in our evolutionary past. The strength of each person's moral intuitions, however, depends greatly on his or her prior learning and experience.

The economist Thomas Sowell describes how differences of opinion on a wide range of social issues are shaped by what he calls conflicting "visions" of human nature. Like Haidt, Sowell describes these visions as "pre-analytic cognitive acts" that we experience before we engage in logical reasoning (Sowell, 2007: 4). Sowell outlines two basic visions. The "constrained" vision is grounded in the belief that people are flawed and therefore incapable of achieving perfection themselves or of engineering a perfect society. Because of our inherent flaws, we need social control mechanisms, such as religion, markets, and government to serve the important role of regulating human behavior to minimize the amount of pain we would otherwise inflict on one another. In this view, social control practices grow gradually out of experience, wisdom, and hard-won lessons over long spans of time. The complex knowledge contained within social control practices is greater than what any single human being can fully comprehend. In Sowell's constrained vision, rapid social change – regardless of the good intentions of those who advocate for it – runs the risk of disrupting longstanding social control solutions, including such things as norms, laws, and institutions, and, in doing so, risks ushering in social disorder and misery.

In contrast, Sowell's unconstrained vision holds that, while people might rightly be considered "flawed," they and the societies they live in can be improved, and perhaps even perfected. In this view, people can use their moral and intellectual powers to design a better world and, in doing so, transform social relations from a default position of selfishness to one of generosity. Those with intellectual acumen and a selfless moral nature can help make better decisions for society, thus eliminating the need to rely on the past as a source of wisdom. In fact, in this view, we *shouldn't* rely on the past, since it contains many social practices that are neither rational nor just. The unconstrained vision thus lends itself to activism that relies on human intelligence, compassion, and empathy and that aims to eliminate what are seen as outdated social practices, mindsets, institutions, and laws.

Building on the work of Haidt and Sowell, the economist Arnold Kling describes how people's intuitions about social problems are shaped by what he calls the "three languages of politics." The three languages function as interpretive lenses through which progressives (i.e., liberals in the United States), conservatives, and libertarians come to identify, support, and condemn the perceived protagonists and antagonists involved in a range of social problems. Progressives use the language of "oppressor/oppressed," which reflects a belief that "certain groups or categories of people intrinsically fall into [one or the other of these] categories" (Kling, 2017: 5). This leads them to see social problems as the result of abuses of power and authority in which oppressors dominate and exploit those with less power.

Conservatives are also concerned about social problems. However, according to Kling, they use the language of "order/chaos," which reflects the view that social problems are the result of a breakdown in traditional values brought on by rebellious individuals and groups who are "indifferent to the assault on the moral virtues and traditions that are the foundation of our civilization" (2017: 4). Conservatives thus tend to resist

8

efforts to alter society too quickly out of a concern over the unintended negative consequences that are likely to occur when flawed human beings attempt to improve a social order that has taken generations to evolve.

Finally, in Kling's description, libertarians use the language of "freedom/constraint," which reflects their inclination to see social problems as a struggle between those who would permit or enable the rights and autonomy of individuals to be sacrificed in service of a higher purpose and those who would resist such efforts. The freedom/constraint lens leads libertarians to oppose policies that would limit or reduce individual freedom of choice and to be especially sensitive to government overreach into the private affairs of citizens.

Table 1.1 shows how the perspectives of Haidt, Sowell, and Kling overlap. Each has something useful to offer as we attempt to understand why contemporary Americans struggle to communicate about social problems. On its own, however, each shines only a narrow spotlight on the nature of the challenge. For instance, one might argue that we should recognize that individuals with

Table 1.1 Three overlapping perspectives

|  | Social Justice | Social Order |
|---|---|---|
| Haidt | Individualizing moral intuitions that put the individual at the center of moral concern | Binding moral intuitions that put social groups at the center of moral concern |
| Sowell | Unconstrained vision of people's ability to improve and perfect social institutions and society | Constrained vision of people's ability to improve and perfect social institutions and society |
| Kling | Oppressor/oppressed lens for interpreting social events | Order/chaos lens for interpreting social events |

strong individualizing moral intuitions are also fully capable of binding themselves into tribal coalitions in order to pursue their social justice aims. Or one could assert that Kling doesn't consider the fact that people's preferences for one narrative language over another may run deep and at times contradict the political label (i.e., progressive, conservative, libertarian) with which they identify. Or one might contend that Sowell's categories (i.e., constrained and unconstrained) are overly abstract and often far removed from the terminology that real-world individuals see themselves reflected in. One might also point out that Sowell's "unconstrained vision" is not only a problem on the left but is rather a problem inherent in most forms of political extremism, regardless of political orientation.

What is needed, therefore, is a framework that both simply and directly organizes the underlying currents of these three frameworks in a way that: (1) is intelligible to people outside of academia; (2) facilitates understanding among people with opposing viewpoints; and (3) is useful to those interested in better understanding how and why twenty-first-century Americans disagree over social problems and their solutions.

We wrote this book to provide such a framework. In it we suggest that a *Social Order* or *Social Justice* orientation, both deeply rooted in moral intuitions, visions, and narrative lenses, underlies Americans' divergent responses to today's most pressing social problems. Proponents of each orientation have distinct ways of experiencing and thinking about human nature, the nature of social systems, social change, empathy, inequality, fairness, rights, responsibilities, agency, and the value of past social practices.

Those with a Social Order orientation tend to believe that human nature contains both good and evil and, importantly, cannot fundamentally change. This makes them wary of efforts to transform society that depend on people becoming more compassionate, generous, or universalistic in their moral concern for others. They observe that most people naturally empathize most strongly with those in their tribe and believe that getting them to do otherwise will always be an uphill climb.

They may further believe that all good things come with a cost, that no society is perfect or perfectible, and that as a result every social system is built on a complex set of tradeoffs. This means, for example, that one should not expect to successfully eradicate all forms of bias from individuals and institutions without at the same time imposing costly and perhaps morally or philosophically undesirable enforcement practices. Because no system is perfect or perfectible, and because of the weight the Social Order perspective places on the lessons of the past, its proponents tend to believe that success is best pursued by working within the existing system rather than attempting to fundamentally reform it or the people who comprise it. In short, those with a Social Order perspective tend to exhibit binding moral intuitions, a constrained vision of human nature, and a tendency to view social problems and solutions in terms of their implications for order and stability in society.

In contrast, those with a Social Justice orientation don't emphasize such constraints. They tend to believe that individuals and society can and should be reformed to make them more equitable and compassionate than they currently are. This encourages them to empathize with those who are marginalized by the current social order and to advocate for social and individual change.

Those with a Social Justice orientation are less willing to accept that transforming a social system involves unwanted tradeoffs and, even when they see such tradeoffs, they are more likely to view them as necessary to achieve their social justice goals. For example, some people with a Social Justice orientation acknowledge that social policies such as affirmative action and social programs such as welfare may not be perfect, but they argue that the laudable goal of social justice justifies the use of less-than-perfect means to achieve it (as in, "to make an omelet, you have to break some eggs"). In short, those with a Social Justice orientation tend to exhibit individualizing moral intuitions, an unconstrained vision of human nature, and a tendency to view social problems and solutions in terms of their implications for the oppressed in society.

## Implications for Social Scientific Research

Opposing sides on any issue often point to empirical studies to support their arguments. This means that social scientific research plays a unique role in our understanding of inequality. It is therefore both necessary and useful to consider how the framework we've outlined shapes our collective understanding of the social world.

The Social Order and Social Justice perspectives reflect not only how we perceive social problems, but also how we understand and think about their causes and solutions. Social scientific research is unrivaled in its ability to help us discern important social facts – such as the extent of demographic change over time or how much poverty there is in a society. But it has only limited power to pinpoint *causal* relationships between phenomena. Few natural experiments exist in the social world that allow us to hold all variables constant except the explanatory one of interest – the analytic approach that most powerfully demonstrates causality. Social science research thus puts us in the unenviable position of having to sift through alternative explanations to account for the particular social facts we observe.

What's more, the explanations we rule out or rule in often are subjective and ideologically driven.

There is thus considerable room for our moral and philosophical worldviews to shape our interpretations of social facts and the relationships among them. Our worldviews are linked to motivated reasoning, the human tendency to interpret data in a way that confirms our view of how the world works. Motivated reasoning helps explain why we struggle to get on the same page regarding the causes of gender inequality, racial inequality, the impact of immigration, and so on, despite having access to the same empirical studies (or facts).

Motivated reasoning doesn't mean that it's impossible to come to a better understanding of the connection between various social phenomena. Throughout this book we discuss many basic claims about the social world on which there is much agreement. But we also recognize that when it comes to inequality the facts aren't always clear and motivated reasoning provides a distinct challenge. This is especially true given the changing nature of the extent and causes of problems within our social, economic, and political systems. In the final analysis, we agree with Daniel Patrick Moynihan's (1983) contention that "Everyone is entitled to his own opinion, but not his own facts." We believe that by better understanding the different perspectives we bring to the data, the more we will be able we to discern the facts.

The challenge of interpreting social science research becomes even more pronounced when the research is being done disproportionately by people with one ideological orientation or another. Because academic research grows and evolves based on a system of peer review, it becomes distorted when the people doing and reviewing the research share the same ideological orientation. When one orientation emerges as dominant, groupthink and confirmation bias grow while resentment festers among those whose views are sidelined.

The Social Justice perspective currently is ascendant in the social sciences because most social scientists locate themselves on the left side of the political spectrum (Abrams, 2016). The orienting concern for many of these scholars is reducing social inequality (Smith, 2014). By contrast, there are few social scientists today whose main concern is understanding or safeguarding the social order (Turner et al., 2012), which means the concerns of most social scientists are out of step with those of the American polity (Turner, 2019). This points to the importance of employing researchers and policymakers with diverse viewpoints to study and address social problems, a point we address at the end of the book.

### *Applying the Social Order–Social Justice Framework*

In the chapters that follow, we apply the Social Order–Social Justice framework to disagreements over a wide variety of topics. As an example of our approach, in the following sections we briefly show how our framework can be applied to both racial inequality, which we return to later in the book, and the COVID-19 pandemic

#### *Racial inequality*

Many commentators with a Social Justice orientation view the existence of racial disparities as a self-evident indictment of the system that is believed to generate them. In other words, the thinking is, but for a flawed, oppressive system that serves the interests of those in power, inequality wouldn't exist. Consider the comments of history professor Ibram X. Kendi when asked about the findings of a study showing considerable racial inequality in patterns of economic mobility: "As an anti-racist, when I see racial disparities, I see racism."

He continues, describing his view of how others might come to a different conclusion:

> But I know for many racist Americans, when they see racial disparities they see black inferiority. So I was not surprised in the least by the number of comments claiming racism is not a major factor in the lives of black males. So many of our neighbors are unfortunately still living in their post-racial fantasy world. Let's hope this study thrusts some of them into the racist real world. (Miller et al., 2018)

Kendi's response and his characterization of his detractors' responses reflects precisely the breakdown in conversation that motivates this book.

In his other written work, Kendi has advocated for addressing racial inequality through race-conscious, affirmative action policies in institutions where there is an unequal representation of groups (Kendi, 2019a). Further, he advocates for the establishment of a new federal Department of Anti-Racism (DOA), "comprised of formally trained experts on racism and no political appointees":

> The DOA would be responsible for preclearing all local, state and federal public policies to ensure they won't yield racial inequity, monitor those policies, investigate private racist policies when racial inequity surfaces, and monitor public officials for expressions of racist ideas. The DOA would be empowered with disciplinary tools to wield over and against policymakers and public officials who do not voluntarily change their racist policy and ideas. (Kendi, 2019b)

To some, the mere suggestion of such a department raises concerns of authoritarianism. Yet, in this view, the goal of social justice (i.e., "making the omelet") more than justifies the means of getting there ("breaking a few eggs").

Many people with a Social Order orientation likely share Kendi's disapproval of racial discrimination, but they may not view it as the only contributing factor when it comes to inequality. They might instead point to the importance of, for example, family structure or the quality of local schools in affecting educational attainment and upward mobility. People with a Social Order orientation might embrace the idea that racial equality is ultimately achieved by grassroots efforts that strengthen institutions and cultural practices that contribute to social order. Ian Rowe, a Resident Fellow at the American Enterprise Institute who has led several efforts aimed at improving educational opportunities for children in underserved communities, has argued that, instead of relying on the federal government to improve the well-being of blacks in the United States, blacks should focus on addressing factors within their control. He writes: "There are pathways to power for young black people. That's why our nation's educators must help black girls and boys cultivate a sense of personal agency and convince them that their deliverance is determined more by their own actions than by the incantations of a newly enlightened majority" (Rowe, 2020).

The approaches of Kendi and Rowe display the Social Justice and Social Order perspectives. Kendi sees the existence of racial inequality as itself proof of social injustice. It stands to reason therefore that, in his view, society must address this injustice through far-reaching social change, and that such change should be engineered by those with the requisite knowledge and moral standing to determine what must be done. Rowe agrees that racism hampers mobility, but he doesn't seek to eliminate all discrimination – which, given the limitations of human nature, may prove difficult or impossible. Instead, he maintains that individuals should seek to gradually elevate themselves through hard work and by building durable institutions, such as strong families and good schools. Rowe's view is that resilience combined with strong community institutions and a success-promoting culture are critical for allowing individuals to flourish and reach their potential. From this perspective, policies such as affirmative action are bound to be ineffective because they do not address the underlying issues that lead to inequality.

To a certain extent, social science research can help map the landscape of inequality. It can establish key facts and trends, such as the extent of racial differences in poverty, income, education and their causes. However, such research – when conducted and presented solely from either a Social Justice or Social Order orientation – is ill-equipped to capture the complex causes of inequality or its potential solutions. There are likely many factors that contribute to inequality, including discrimination, the legacy of unjust practices, human and social capital differences, residential segregation, and cultural values, to name a few. Those with a Social Justice orientation often spotlight especially the first of these factors, while those with a Social Order orientation often spotlight the latter. In the following chapters we discuss these differences and their consequences in more detail.

## The COVID-19 pandemic

As COVID-19 swept through the United States in early 2020, many people responded with shock and bewilderment – little was known about it, including how it was transmitted. The initial response in many places included lockdowns. People were urged to stay inside for all nonessential activity and schools and places of business were closed. Hand sanitizers and disinfectant wipes were in high demand, as people believed they could catch COVID by touching infected surfaces (Tyko, 2020). In the weeks and months that followed we learned more about the virus, including that it was transmitted mainly through the air and in indoor spaces and that it was much more deadly among the elderly than the young. Vaccines were developed and distributed by the late fall of 2020 – much more quickly than anyone, including health experts, anticipated (Lewis, 2021).

At first Americans were largely united in the effort to "flatten the curve." People stayed at home to reduce transmission and to prevent hospitals and the health-care system from being overwhelmed. It wasn't long, however, before debates flared about lockdowns, masking, and how quickly to reopen schools and businesses. President Trump and other conservative politicians settled on the message that the United States would need to accept the virus, reopen schools, and restart the economy. Meanwhile, more progressive politicians favored stricter policies, including prolonged economic shutdowns, limits on in-person gatherings, and mask mandates (Scott, 2020; VanDusky-Allen and Shvetsova, 2021).

Why the divide? We hold that the Social Order–Social Justice framework explains the differences in approaches. As discussed earlier, those with a Social Justice perspective seek to minimize harm and believe that people are capable of using their moral and intellectual powers to better the world. In the case of the COVID-19 response, this had several implications. It meant that we could rely on the technical knowledge of health-care experts to fashion policies to prevent the spread of infection. It also meant that we could trust our fellow citizens to mask up, get vaccinated, and avoid socializing in crowded, indoor places – including schools and places of worship – where the virus was most likely to spread. Such approaches were pursued in the name of protecting the most vulnerable.

Illustrating this perspective, Emily Newman, writing for the online magazine *The Humanist*, listed ten reasons to wear a mask, including altruism, empathy, peace and social justice, responsibility, and service and participation. In the entry for peace and social justice, she explained, "I am fortunate to have good health care, the ability to work from home, and a supportive local network to help me if I get COVID. I wear a mask to protect those more vulnerable to COVID due to lack of community, health issues, and financial burdens caused by lost work time or unemployment, hospital bills, and unforeseen expenses" (Newman 2021).

Those from the Social Order perspective, in contrast, are wary of efforts to transform society, especially if it depends on people becoming more compassionate or generous. They believe that people are imperfect, and society is not perfectible. Efforts to change people and society for the better, even in the name of minimizing harm, therefore come with tradeoffs. With regard to the response to COVID-19, this meant that those from a Social Order perspective were alarmed by the potential for negative long-term consequences of lockdowns and other COVID-19 policy responses. In essence, they were willing to endure more people dying in the short run in order to, as they saw it, preserve the social order that would save lives and maximize well-being over the long run. For example, George Leef, writing in the conservative *National Review*, argued that:

> Government policies almost always have unseen, unintended, and unhappy consequences ... That's as true about Covid policy as anything else. Those who

demanded and got heavy-handed lockdowns and vaccine mandates never bothered to think about the possibility that their approaches might have severe adverse consequences. They were (and remain) hostile toward anyone who argued that they were doing more harm than good. Now it is becoming increasingly evident that the authoritarian "zero Covid" obsession has done immense social damage. Consider, e.g., this story in Canada's National Post by Sabrina Maddeaux, "Lockdowns are Killing Young Canadians." (Leef 2022)

The linked article describes how there was an excess of deaths among young Canadians not directly from COVID-19 but from knock-on causes such as drug overdoses and suicide (Maddeaux, 2021).

Responses to the COVID-19 pandemic exemplify the moral reasoning behind the two perspectives, and because the long-term effects of any large-scale societal response are difficult to discern, we will likely continue to debate policy alternatives to COVID and other possible pandemics in the coming years.

### A Few Caveats

Before we proceed, a few caveats are in order. First, we recognize that, in practice, most people's moral and philosophical leanings are not wholly dominated by either a Social Order or Social Justice orientation and that in the real world there may be elements of each grafted to the other, both in terms of people's goals and the means they prefer for achieving their goals.

Second, people's moral and philosophical leanings can change, either due to their life experiences or other kinds of learning. This is akin to popular sayings that apply to political ideology such as "a conservative is a liberal who's been mugged" or "a liberal is a conservative who's been arrested." It is likely, for instance, that many people were moved to care more about Social Justice issues after the murder of George Floyd. Conversely, others may have shifted their view to Social Order after the riots in the summer of 2020. So while many people's leanings remain fixed over their lifetimes, others may experience some kind of moral or philosophical "awakening" in one direction or another.

Third, our application of the Social Order–Social Justice framework pertains to disagreements about inequality in the United States in the early twenty-first century. In other words, we envision an individual with a Social Order orientation as being protective of the social order as it currently exists. Similarly, we see an individual with a Social Justice orientation as being concerned with injustices as they are defined in the current era. In other words, we recognize that the Social Order or Social Justice perspectives will align with different goals depending on when and where someone lives.

In the late nineteenth century, for example, one of the principal social justice concerns of the women's movement was securing the right to vote. Meanwhile, in the early twenty-first century, one of the principal social justice concerns of the women's movement is protecting bodily autonomy and ending sexual harassment.

Of course, people's desire for change also depends on how well the situation they find themselves in matches their view of how things should be. The greater the disconnect, the more likely people are to get involved in actively seeking change, either through voting or through more intensive activities. Because of this, people's willingness to get involved will vary as the problems they are concerned about improve or worsen, so that, as progress is made, people may become less "involved" in an issue.

Finally, it's important to note that sometimes people agree on which social goals to pursue but disagree on the best way to achieve them. For instance, most of us can agree that we would like to see the prevalence of racism in society driven toward zero. However, people can and do disagree about whether the best way to get there is by adopting a race-conscious approach that seeks to reduce inequality by deliberately taking into account people's racial identities in decision-making (such as in college admission) or by adopting a color-blind approach that seeks to reduce discrimination and increase social harmony by deemphasizing race. The difference in approaches is something we discuss throughout the book.

In short, we believe that because many people gravitate toward either the Social Justice or Social Order perspective when defining and responding to social problems, providing a language and a framework to discuss this dynamic – as we do in this book – can help move conversations forward. The Social Order–Social Justice framework captures a large portion of variation across individuals and groups in their attitudes toward inequality and does so using terms that are meaningful to people inside and outside of academia. Therefore, in the remainder of this book, we treat the Social Justice and Social Order perspectives as distinct, while recognizing that particular individuals and groups may combine them to varying degrees.

### Summary and Plan of the Book

The goal of this book is to show how the Social Order–Social Justice framework can be used to understand the various fault lines that divide contemporary Americans in their views on a variety of social problems, including why we tend to talk past one another, and how we might learn to better appreciate, understand, and respect the moral and philosophical underpinnings of one another's perspectives. In this chapter, we introduced the framework and briefly described how it can be applied to racial and ethnic inequality and disagreement over the best COVID-19 response.

In the next chapter we provide a detailed description of the values, beliefs, and intuitions that align with each side of the framework. We argue that the Social Order and Social Justice perspectives reflect divergent views regarding fairness and equality; freedom, choice, and responsibility; individual and group-based morality; and social change.

In subsequent chapters, we apply the Social Order–Social Justice framework to disagreements about gender inequality, racial inequality, income inequality, and immigration policy. In each chapter, we examine how the values, beliefs, and intuitions contained within the Social Order and Social Justice perspectives drive disagreements about the causes, consequences, and solutions to these problems, and the likely effects of different social policy approaches. By describing the Social Order–Social Justice framework in detail in Chapter 2, and providing several examples of how it can be used in subsequent chapters, we hope that readers will gain a better sense of how to apply its logic to an even larger array of social issues, such as criminal justice, climate change, and drug policy. We conclude with a series of observations and recommendations for improving how we disagree with one another so that our disagreements can become more productive.

# 2

# The Social Order–Social Justice Framework

In the previous chapter, we proposed that a Social Order–Social Justice framework is useful for understanding why twenty-first-century Americans disagree about social problems. In this chapter, we describe the intuitions, values and beliefs that characterize each side of this framework, focusing in particular on their divergent views regarding: fairness and equality; freedom, choice, and responsibility; individual and group-based morality; and social change. These elements do not necessarily constitute a coherent theoretical system within the minds of those to whom they appeal, but rather are invoked and combined as needed in an ongoing process of sense-making when social problems are considered. A core premise of this book is that the result of this sense-making most often bears the stamp of either a Social Order or a Social Justice perspective.

Before describing the specific intuitions and beliefs that characterize the Social Order–Social Justice framework, it is important that we make clear what the framework is and is not meant to explain. The Social Order–Social Justice framework is meant to explain why Americans *today* disagree about social problems. Our core argument is that disagreements arise when fundamentally different ways of interpreting human nature and the nature of social systems come into conflict with one another. We observe that in recent decades such differences have taken on a clear and discernible pattern of polarity.

As we argue below, those with a Social Justice perspective tend to measure fairness in terms of equal *outcomes*, while those with a Social Order perspective tend to measure fairness in terms of uniformly applied *processes*. Those with a Social Justice perspective tend to measure freedom in terms of *power and influence*, while those with a Social Order perspective tend to measure freedom in terms of *options and opportunities*. Those with a Social Justice perspective tend to draw on moral intuitions that emphasize *care for the vulnerable*, while those with a Social Order perspective tend to draw on moral intuitions that also emphasize *group loyalty* and *respect for authority*. Finally, those with a Social Justice perspective tend to be *enthusiastic* about implementing social change, while those with a Social Order perspective tend to be *cautious* about doing so. These polarities go a long way toward explaining why disagreements about social problems persist and why solutions tend to be elusive. These differences are summarized in Table 2.1.

The Social Order–Social Justice framework is meant to explain disagreements over problems of inequality in the contemporary United States. It is not meant to explain disagreements about inequality that were salient in the US during other historical eras or to explain disagreements about social problems in other cultural milieus. For example, in the US today, those with a Social Justice perspective seem willing to condone restricting free speech in the name of anti-racism, while during the McCarthy era, those with a Social Order perspective were willing to condone restricting free speech in the name of anti-communism. It appears that

**Table 2.1** The Social Order and Social Justice framework

|  | Fairness & Equality | Freedom, Choice & Responsibility | Individual & Group-Based Morality | Social Change |
|---|---|---|---|---|
| Social Order emphasizes ... | Equal opportunity | Options and opportunities | Group loyalty and respect for authority | Slow, incremental change |
| Social Justice emphasizes ... | Equal outcomes | Power and influence | Care for the vulnerable | Extensive change |

both sides are capable of prioritizing ideological goals (i.e., anti-racism and anti-communism) over fidelity to a core democratic principle (i.e., free speech) when doing so aligns with their interests. In other words, there's nothing inherent in the Social Order or Social Justice perspectives that makes one favor fairness in terms of outcomes and the other favor fairness in terms of evenly applied processes. The framework, therefore, is not meant to "essentialize" proponents of either perspective in that we do *not* claim that the values, beliefs, or moral intuitions that *currently* characterize each side of the Social Order–Social Justice framework always have or always will characterize them. Instead, we claim that the Social Order–Social Justice heuristic, as described in this book, is useful because it captures much of the variation in how *contemporary Americans* think about social problems.

## Fairness and Equality

Everyone is concerned with fairness. But people differ in what they consider fair. In the contemporary US, a person with a Social Justice perspective tends to measure fairness in terms of *outcomes*, while a person with a Social Order perspective tends to measure fairness in terms of *processes*. Equality is essential for both perspectives, but the two groups see equality differently. The person with a Social Order perspective favors equal treatment in selection processes for jobs, schools, sports positions, and the like. Equality-of-process is achieved by ensuring that selection standards are applied uniformly to all individuals. If this occurs, the person with a Social Order perspective will feel that fairness has been achieved, regardless of the outcome. For example, from a Social Order perspective, a fair selection process can result in a talented or qualified manager receiving several promotions in a single year, while other managers receive none.

As long as the criteria for promotion were applied equally to all eligible employees, fairness was achieved. Fairness, thus conceived, contributes to the Social Order by anchoring selection processes in clearly defined, uniformly applied standards that lend validity and authority to the outcomes they produce. To achieve such fairness, selection processes that focus on performance-related characteristics and are "blind" to immutable characteristics (i.e., race, gender, social class, or sexual orientation) are preferred. Due to the emphasis on "blind" process, from a Social Order perspective, fairness and *in*equality are not necessarily opposed. That is, a blind selection process may yield outcomes that are unequal on several dimensions and still be considered fair.

27

Why We Disagree about Inequality

A person with a Social Justice perspective, on the other hand, tends to measure fairness by the extent to which groups are rewarded equally – that is proportionally – in societal level competitions for resources, including wealth, status, power, heath, and happiness. Equality is thus conceived as the achievement of proportionality in the distribution of *outcomes* across social groups. For example, from a Social Justice perspective, a fair manager-selection process would result in the promotion of managers whose characteristics, such as race, gender, social class, or sexual orientation, match the distribution of these characteristics in the general population. As long as the selection process produces such a match, a person with a Social Justice perspective will be satisfied that fairness has been achieved.

If, for whatever reason, the selection process does not yield such a match, then it is likely to be considered unfair and in need of modification. In other words, even if the process *appears* to be fair (i.e., uniform or blind), the fact that it produced unequal outcomes suggests that one group must have had an unfair advantage over others. This could occur through their having greater access to the opportunity in the first place or because of the use of assessment criteria that favor one group over another. Fairness, thus conceived, contributes to Social Justice by ensuring that: (1) no disadvantaged social group is left behind in the competition for resources; and (2) no advantaged group reaps more than its allotted share of social benefits, as measured by its numerical representation in the population. To achieve such fairness, "non-blind" selection processes that explicitly consider immutable characteristics are preferred. Due to the emphasis on outcomes, fairness and inequality are here viewed as being in direct opposition to one another. In other words, from a Social Justice perspective, a truly fair process should never result in unequal (that is, disproportional) outcomes across social groups.

Because of their different definitions of what's fair, the Social Order and Social Justice perspectives are both vulnerable to charges of *un*fairness" within contemporary US culture. The Social Order perspective is "unfair" because it favors a "blind" selection process that, under conditions of societal inequality, perpetuates an unequal distribution of resources, such as promotions, money, influence, or power, among social groups. The Social Justice perspective is "unfair" because it favors the distribution of such resources based at least in part on immutable characteristics that are unrelated to merit. Regarding race, for example, the former perspective is often criticized for permitting "colorblind racism," where the realities of racial disparities are dismissed or downplayed, while the latter is often criticized for permitting "reverse discrimination," where individuals belonging to groups known to have been discriminated against are given preferential treatment over historically dominant groups.

These disparate notions of fairness explain why proponents of each perspective tend to view the other as hypocritical and immoral. The person with a Social Justice perspective might ask: "How can you say you care about fairness when you favor a selection process that perpetuates social inequalities?" The person with a Social Order perspective might ask: "How can you say you care about fairness when you favor a selection process that takes into account immutable characteristics instead of relying solely on merit and skill?" Worse still, by failing to recognize as "moral" the fairness goals inherent in each other's position, the motivation of each to engage in civil discourse with the other is reduced.

## *Freedom, Choice, and Responsibility*

Most people in the contemporary US are concerned with freedom. But people differ in how they define what it means to be free. A person with a Social Justice perspective tends to measure freedom in terms of *power and influence*, while a person with a Social Order perspective tends to measure freedom in terms of *options and opportunities*. Both perspectives are concerned with the ability of individuals to make choices, but their views of the scope of those choices differ.

The person with a Social Order perspective wants to ensure that people have the choice to *pursue* opportunities for well-being and success within the larger system. Results of such pursuits may vary based on an individual's talent, taste, values, ambition, and effort. From this perspective, individuals are the primary causal agent of the outcomes they experience. Success depends on their ability to seize available opportunities and avoid the pitfalls inherent in competing for success in social life. Moreover, because differences in individual and group outcomes are believed to result mostly from differences in individual inputs, such outcomes are considered, by their very nature, legitimate. Freedom of choice, from this perspective, implies the freedom to choose which opportunities to pursue and with what degree of effort. This view legitimizes the current social order by attributing the most social inequality to individual differences in, for instance, talent, taste, effort, and preferences.

Meanwhile, a person with a Social Justice perspective tends to measure freedom in terms of *power and influence*. This person wants to ensure that people have the freedom to achieve well-being and success and that society does not systematically inhibit them from doing so. Individuals are assumed to be equally endowed at birth with talent and motivation, and society is assumed to be structured in such a way as to help or hinder them in converting their talent and motivation into well-being and success. Therefore, variation in outcomes across individuals and groups is interpreted as being due to discrimination or privilege, rather than to individual differences in talent, taste, effort, and preferences. Freedom, from this perspective, means *freedom from discrimination and oppression*, so that when it comes to explaining inequality, society and its discriminatory practices are viewed as the primary causal agents of unequal outcomes. This view of freedom, as freedom from discrimination, legitimizes the need for social justice activism.

Within the contemporary US, the Social Order and Social Justice perspectives are both criticized for being out of touch with the reality of social life. The Social Justice perspective is criticized for downplaying individual agency in favor of blaming social structures for individual failures (and successes). Critics argue that this fosters a *victim mentality* in which people's failures (and successes) are viewed as the result of structural oppression (and privilege). In contrast, the Social Order perspective is criticized for downplaying structural discrimination (and privilege) and blaming (and crediting) individuals for their failures (and successes), thereby fostering a *blame-the-victim mentality*, particularly when failure is the outcome.

Regarding racial inequality, for example, an advocate of the Social Order perspective may be criticized for downplaying the effects of structural racism while emphasizing the role of individual responsibility in negative life outcomes, thereby blaming the victim. In contrast, an advocate of the Social Justice perspective may be criticized for downplaying the role of individual agency in achievement (such as studying and working hard), thereby fostering a victim mentality emphasizing disempowerment and passivity.

A key difference in these perspectives lies in their conceptions of freedom and its role in producing desirable life outcomes. The Social Order perspective emphasizes the freedom *to* choose from among existing options in pursuing success, while the Social Justice perspective emphasizes freedom *from* oppression as a necessary and sufficient condition for achieving success.

These disparate notions of freedom help explain why, within the contemporary US, proponents of both perspectives tend to view each other as misguided. A person with a Social Justice perspective might ask: "How can you say you care about freedom when you downplay the role of *oppression* in limiting people's opportunities?" The person with a Social Order perspective might ask: "How can you say you care about freedom when you downplay the role of *individual choice and agency* in enabling people to pursue success?" Worse still, by using the same terms (freedom, choice, responsibility, and oppression) and applying them differently, the ability of each side to engage in meaningful discourse with the other is severely constrained.

## Individual and Group-Based Morality

Over a decade of research in the field of moral psychology supports the conclusion that the urge to care for the vulnerable and safeguard individual welfare is supported by universally held moral intuitions (Haidt, 2012). In other words, people from all political orientations value caring for others. Where people differ, however, is in the degree to which they also feel an intuitive urge to show loyalty to groups, respect authority, and honor social practices of the past, that is, to safeguard the welfare of the organizations and institutions that comprise the social order. This difference has important implications for understanding the Social Order–Social Justice framework.

Within the contemporary US, people whose moral intuitions focus largely or exclusively on caring for others are particularly attuned to the plight of the vulnerable and the rights of the oppressed. Their focus on *individual welfare* leads them to interpret social problems as the result of unequal or unfair treatment by those with the power to behave otherwise. In contrast, those whose moral intuitions encompass a concern with *group welfare* believe that people should behave in ways that strengthen social cohesion by strengthening families, communities, and nations. They believe that strong institutions and groups are necessary for regulating and channeling individual desire and self-interest toward collectively valuable ends. The moral intuitions of those with a Social Order perspective thus lead them to view social problems as indicative of a breakdown in regulatory forces, including norms, obligations, roles, or the rule of law, and to conceptualize solutions in terms of strengthening these elements.

Within the contemporary US, the unique clusters of moral intuitions associated with the Social Order and Social Justice perspectives often lead their adherents to favor different social policies. For example, the emphasis on care and fairness motivates someone with a Social Justice perspective to be greatly concerned with the suffering of others, especially when those others are members of vulnerable or marginalized groups. This emphasis lends urgency to goals such as protecting individual rights and liberating the vulnerable from oppression. It also leads those with a Social Justice perspective to moralize disadvantage by: (1) viewing as immoral those who treat disadvantage as an inevitable tradeoff in the pursuit of other social goods; and (2) viewing lower-status members of society unquestioningly as victims who are morally worthy of care and protection. Morality thus conceived contributes to Social Justice by leading its proponents to recognize as virtuous those who stand up for the rights of the oppressed. To behave morally is, from the Social Justice perspective, to dedicate oneself to bringing about a world in which inequality, oppression, and suffering are greatly reduced or eliminated, and to support social policies aimed at achieving such goals.

Someone with a Social Order perspective, on the other hand, tends to be concerned with both the welfare of individuals *and* the welfare of groups and institutions. This broader base of moral concerns leads them to emphasize virtues such as self-restraint, duty, loyalty, and the performance of group-based roles and obligations, all of which enable social groups and the larger social system to operate in a smooth and orderly fashion. These group-focused virtues exist alongside other virtues, such as liberty and self-expression, which enable individuals to pursue their own self-fulfillment, albeit within limits.

In addition to emphasizing *rights* that protect individuals from unnecessary social constraints (such as the right to own property, the right to bear arms, and the right to a fair trial), the Social Order perspective also emphasizes *responsibilities and obligations* that bind individuals to groups. These include respecting authority figures such as parents, teachers, police, and public servants; serving one's country in times of threat; honoring social practices of the past; and accepting restrictions on one's behavior based on family, community, national, and religious affiliations. Morality, thus conceived, contributes to the Social Order by recognizing as virtuous those who are willing to subordinate their personal desires to the needs and expectations of institutions and groups. To behave morally is, from the Social Order perspective, to balance one's individual rights and desires against one's group-based responsibilities and obligations.

Unsurprisingly, each of these moral perspectives is vulnerable to criticism. The Social Justice perspective is often criticized for putting the desires of individuals before the expectations of groups, while the Social Order perspective is often criticized for doing the opposite. With regards to the family, for example, those with a Social Justice perspective are more likely to support single women choosing to have children out of wedlock and less likely to view such choices as being bad for society, whereas those with a Social Order perspective are more likely to express the opposite view (Pew Research Center, 2010). Together, these different moral intuitions lead to divergent views as to how best to balance the desires of individuals against the needs of groups. By extension, they also lead to a favoring of different personal and policy approaches when individual and group interests diverge.

Another point of tension between individual and group-based moral perspectives involves the degree to which one's moral responsibilities apply beyond one's ingroup. Those with a Social Justice perspective tend toward a *universalistic* morality characterized by impartiality toward the beneficiaries of one's moral concerns. From this perspective, one has a moral obligation to care about the welfare of others, regardless of who they are or where they come from. To be moral is to be *non-selective* in the application of one's morality, and thus to aim for the widest possible scope of moral inclusion. This tendency toward moral universalism and inclusivity inclines those with a Social Justice perspective to think of themselves as "citizens of the world," rather than as members of particular communities or nations, and to think of their moral responsibilities as applying to all of humanity.

Those with a Social Order perspective, on the other hand, tend toward a *parochial* view of morality characterized by *selectivity* in the enactment of moral behavior. Their morality tracks the old adage, "Charity begins at home." This view assumes that resources are limited and that their distribution requires prioritization. From this perspective, it is one's primary moral obligation to provide for the well-being of those within one's ingroup, be it their family, church, or country, and only after the needs of one's ingroup have been met, to extend one's moral resources further. This tendency toward moral parochialism inclines those with a Social Order perspective to feel less moral regard for those outside of their social orbit. For example, a person with a Social Order perspective may be more inclined to donate money to feed the hungry in their own community than in a foreign country.

We can see these differences play out in attitudes toward US immigration policy. The inclusive, universalistic moral intuitions of those with a Social Justice perspective incline them toward loosening restrictions to enable those seeking a better life in the US to achieve it, regardless of their country of origin. Meanwhile, the more parochial, ingroup-focused moral intuitions of those with a Social Order perspective incline them toward maintaining or increasing immigration restrictions in order to prioritize and safeguard the well-being of US citizens, even though doing so may limit the well-being of prospective immigrants.

By favoring different aspects of the tradeoff between the needs of individuals and the needs of groups, proponents of the Social Order and Social Justice perspectives often fail to understand one another's moral motivations and priorities. They are thus more likely to view one another's policy proposals as morally misguided when discussing social problems such as immigration. We develop this point further in Chapter 6.

## Social Change

Finally, while proponents of the Social Order and Social Justice perspectives both see room for improvement in existing social systems, they tend to differ in the type of social change they think is most needed and how best to achieve it. This tendency is rooted in two interrelated factors: (1) trust in the wisdom of the past versus trust in humankind's ability to improve upon it; and (2) the desire for sweeping versus incremental social change.

Both the Social Order and Social Justice perspectives recognize that social systems are complex in their functions. However, they differ with respect to their belief in people's ability to improve upon or perfect existing social systems without bringing forth unintended negative consequences.

Those with a Social Order perspective, for example, are skeptical of humankind's ability to reshape social systems intentionally and successfully. Their respect for past social practices reflects an underlying belief that *social systems make people good* by imparting traditions that contain within them a wisdom that surpasses that of any individual, regardless of how smart or insightful that individual is. Existing social systems are understood as "natural" in an evolutionary sense, in that they embody countless generations of accumulated knowledge and experience. Those with a Social Order perspective are thus hesitant to alter, let alone overhaul, such systems.

They are especially hesitant when the goals of social change originate in trends in social thought that strive for a utopia – trends often found in social movements aimed at eliminating inequality and achieving economic prosperity for all. Their skepticism of utopian social policy goals and of humankind's ability to implement them is also rooted in the belief that a social system free from disparity and conflicts of interest is, in practice, unattainable. They tend to believe that it is within the very nature of complex systems to operate by means of "tradeoffs" rather than "solutions." From this "constrained" perspective, attempts to achieve utopian social goals (i.e., "solutions") are not only doomed to fail, but are likely to make matters worse (Sowell, 2007). In this context, it is preferable for human beings to cultivate respect for past social practices and traditions and for the social systems from which they emerged, and to endeavor to reform them incrementally and with the greatest of caution lest they generate "chaos" in the form of unintended negative consequences (Kling, 2017). It is in this sense that proponents of the Social Order perspective may be considered "conservative."

Those with a Social Justice perspective, on the other hand, are optimistic about the ability of humankind to improve existing social systems without bringing about unintended negative consequences. They believe that *people make social systems good.* Their optimism in this regard is fueled in part by skepticism toward past social practices and traditions. As a result, those with a Social Justice perspective tend to view many current cultural practices as vestiges of prior generations' attempts to organize their social worlds without the benefit of modern moral and scientific understanding. These past attempts at social organization are viewed as causing the very disadvantages that the Social Justice perspective seeks to eradicate, including vastly unequal distributions of resources, enormously unequal social statuses among people of different races, religions, and lifestyles, and untold numbers of abuses, oppressions, and atrocities.

Those with a Social Justice perspective are thus eager to reform, if not overhaul, existing social systems in order to improve the lives of those who have suffered – and would continue to suffer – under them. They are especially eager to orient social systems toward idealistic goals, such as eliminating inequality and achieving economic prosperity for all. Given the unprecedented state of wealth and scientific knowledge in the world, they believe such goals have never been more within reach. As a result, they are less inclined to view "trade-offs" as an inevitable feature of social life, preferring instead to pursue "solutions" aimed at bringing about their vision of a better world (Sowell, 2007). They believe that humankind's ability to overcome obstacles (to achieving a better world) is limited mainly by the strength of people's commitment to the goal. From a Social Justice perspective, it is imperative to reject past social practices and replace them with better ones so that social progress may be maintained. It is in this sense that proponents of the Social Justice perspective may be considered "progressive."

The Social Justice and Social Order perspectives also differ with regard to their desire for immediate versus incremental social change. To the degree that the unwelcomed outcomes of social systems involve oppression and suffering, and in light of the Social Justice perspective's optimism regarding humankind's ability to improve upon such systems, the person with a Social Justice perspective often feels a powerful sense of urgency in addressing social problems. As a common Social Justice call-and-response protest chant succinctly states: "What do we want? Change! When do we want it? Now!"

From this perspective, there is no acceptable reason to delay helping people who are suffering. In contrast, from a Social Order perspective, rapid social change is undesirable, even when its goal is to reduce hardship. Regardless of the social problem to be solved, the person with a Social Order perspective tends to believe that the social system from which it emerged contains accumulated wisdom. This wisdom is seen as the result of generations of trial and error during which a complex balance of competing interests has been achieved. From a Social Order perspective, such complexity can never provide a perfect outcome for every individual or group, but it can provide a good *overall* outcome, given the enduring nature of competing interests. Therefore, from a Social Order perspective, any attempt to reengineer social systems should be pursued cautiously and incrementally in order to minimize the likely emergence of unintended consequences.

*Conclusion*

Social *in*justice and social *dis*order are perennial threats to society that can manifest in a wide range of social problems. To solve such problems, social policies are needed that honor the assumptions and concerns of both the Social Justice and Social Order perspectives. Before such policies can be formulated, however, a clearer understanding of the nature of the disagreement between them is needed.

In the following chapters, we use the Social Order–Social Justice framework to address the question of why contemporary Americans disagree about specific social problems. We focus on gender inequality, racial and ethnic inequality, income inequality, and immigration policy. We describe these problems in detail and analyze them based on the moral and philosophical beliefs and priorities contained within the Social Justice and Social Order perspectives. We then discuss how these divergent beliefs and priorities produce opposing perspectives on the causes and consequences of each social problem. We also address specific policy proposals with an eye toward understanding where and why the Social Justice and Social Order perspectives diverge.

# 3

# Gender Inequality

Gender inequality takes many forms and can be measured in a variety of ways. One of the most frequently discussed indicators is the earnings gap. In 2019, among full-time year-round workers, women earned about 82 percent of what men did. This figure is up from about 60 percent in 1980, indicating a narrowing of the gap over time (US Census Bureau, 2019). Nevertheless, a substantial difference remains.

Some see this persistent gap as evidence of social injustice, reflecting gender-based discriminatory behavior women face across their lifetimes. As professors Anthony Carnevale and Nicole Smith argued in *Time* magazine:

> Closing the gender wage gap will require initiatives aimed at combatting workplace discrimination. One of these is the Paycheck Fairness Act, which would increase wage transparency and provide legal protections for workers who raise concerns about gender-based wage discrimination. It will also require flexible work options, which build upon women's rights established under the Family and Medical Leave Act and assuage the slowdown in women's career trajectories when they decide to start a family. It will also require us to alter the cultural norms

and stereotypes we communicate to young girls, through the stories we tell and the people we admire, about what is possible for them. (Carnevale and Smith, 2014)

While some scholars – primarily from the Social Justice perspective – argue that systemic discrimination is the key cause of gender inequality, others – mainly from the Social Order perspective – point out that it's not the only factor worthy of attention. Regarding the pay gap, those from the Social Order perspective hold that it is at least partly due to the choices men and women make about what they study in college, which careers they pursue, and the roles they choose to occupy as parents. As economists Mark Perry and Andrew Biggs assert, "The reality is that men and women make very different career and work choices, and frequently play very different family roles, especially for families with children. While gender discrimination undoubtedly occurs, it is individuals' choice – not discrimination – which accounts for the vast majority of gender differences in earnings" (Perry and Biggs, 2018).

The assertion that individual choices based on underlying preferences play a role in explaining the gender pay gap raises the question, which is the bigger contributor? If the more powerful determinant is choices, then attempts to engineer a different kind of outcome – for example, by limiting access to jobs for men in order to create opportunities for women – may be counterproductive and make men and women – and, by extension, their children and communities – worse off. Someone with a Social Order orientation might hold that, while it is natural to expect that the social roles of men and women will change over time in response to changing economic conditions, such as rising living standards and the changing nature of work, such change is best if it occurs gradually and organically via the choices that individuals make rather than via policy interventions. With a slower pace, the thinking goes, social change is enabled while social order is preserved.

It's important to remember that many individuals don't adhere wholly to a Social Justice or Social Order perspective and that, often, holders of both viewpoints acknowledge that discrimination *and* individual choices might play a role in gender inequality. But the two perspectives emphasize different factors as primary causes and solutions. And when considering empirical evidence, they tend to rely on different sources to support their positions or, when they rely on the same sources, they tend to interpret them differently.

To anchor our discussion of disagreements about gender inequality and the ways in which the Social Order and Social Justice perspectives contribute to such disagreements today, we first provide a brief historical overview of the changing roles of men and women in society.

### Historical Overview of the Changing Roles of Men and Women

Proponents of the Social Justice perspective often highlight the ways in which patriarchal societies limit women's choices. The roots of this line of thought in Western societies go back centuries. For example, feminist writing in the 1780s and 1790s grew out of debates about liberty in the context of the American and French revolutions.

The feminist movement in the United States since the nineteenth century is often divided into waves. These waves reflect the historical conditions in which they emerged. First-wave feminism focused on women's political equality, and particularly on the right to vote.

It extended from the mid 1800s until 1920, when the 19th Amendment finally secured this right.

This first wave occurred during a period of profound economic and social change. Before industrialization, which in the United States began in the 1800s, the US population was primarily rural and agrarian and most men and women worked around the home. As the market economy grew, so did the number of people who worked outside the home for pay. At first it was primarily men, but by the end of the nineteenth century a growing number of women entered the labor market. These women were generally young and unmarried, and worked in low-skill jobs as domestics, laundresses, and manufacturing pieceworkers (Goldin, 1990). Women's labor force participation continued to expand through the early to mid-twentieth century into office and clerical work. Although these positions were of higher status than previous options, they brought little possibility for promotion (Goldin, 2006). More generally, first-wave feminism arose during a time when an agrarian society was giving way to a more urban, industrial, and affluent one. In this new society, women increasingly took on roles outside their families and sought corresponding individual and political rights commensurate with those roles.

Second-wave feminism, which spanned from about 1960 to 1990, focused on increasing economic opportunities for women. It also popularized the notion of "gender," including socially prescribed gender roles in the home and workplace that served to reinforce inequality. During this second wave, activists pushed for equal access to jobs and for equal pay for equal work.

These pursuits once again occurred alongside changing economic and social conditions. An increasing number of women entered the paid labor force as the twentieth century progressed, though women continued to be the secondary earners in their households. Upward mobility in most women's jobs remained limited, and labor force participation rates for women with young children remained low into the 1970s (Costa, 2000; Goldin, 1990). Economic historian Claudia Goldin (2006) calls the period since the late 1970s – up through and including the present – the "quiet revolution." During this time a growing number of married women with young children remained in the labor market, social norms about the balancing of family and career changed, and women became more highly represented in well-paying professional jobs that previously had been occupied by men, such as doctors, lawyers, and managers. Second-wave feminists thus sought equality in the labor market as women's paid work became a more central feature of their lives.

"Third-wave feminism," which began around 1990, emerged from a sense that previous waves focused too much on the concerns of upper-middle-class white women. Partly in response, third-wave feminism emphasized how women face different kinds of inequality depending on their social and economic positions. The movement also focused on *intersectionality*, where women may face multiple disadvantages due not only to their gender, but also to their race, class, and sexual orientation. Judith Butler, a theorist who influenced third-wave feminism, wrote about how women and men, taught by parents, friends, and the culture at large, *perform* gender, and thus reinforce existing gender stereotypes and behaviors (Butler, 1999). The third wave of feminism sought to correct the perceived narrowness of previous waves and expand feminist goals to include a broader array of women. The third wave also argued that inequality was not entirely due to overt discrimination, but was partly due to specific family and work patterns that could be traced to the different ways that men and women are socialized (Kinser, 2004).

Each wave of feminism was met by opposition in some quarters. While it is beyond the scope of this book to fully describe the contours of these debates, suffice it to say that opponents were often concerned that women's new roles were challenging familiar and established ways of life (Mendes, 2011).

More generally, the benefits of industrialization and the rising standards of living it produced freed women and men from traditional community and familial relationships and constraints. These changes allowed for a focus on personal autonomy and the pursuit of individual freedoms that would have been impossible for most people centuries earlier. These broad changes enabled Social Justice proponents to argue that the traditional limitations placed on women were no longer justified – if they ever were – and that they violated Enlightenment principles concerning life, liberty, and the pursuit of happiness.

Even with unprecedented historical declines in gender inequality, debates persist about the causes of gender disparities and how to address them. The Social Justice–Social Order heuristic can help describe the contours of these debates. Our discussion focuses on the different intuitions about fairness and equality; freedom, choice, and responsibility; individual and group-based morality; and attitudes toward social change that are characteristic of each perspective.

### *Fairness and Equality*

Because the Social Justice perspective today sees fairness primarily in terms of equal outcomes, the fact that men and women differ in their earnings is considered strong

**Figure 3.1**  Women's median annual earnings as a percent of men's earnings for full-time, year-round workers, 1960–2020

*Source:* Data from US Census Bureau, 2020f

evidence that social institutions unfairly favor men over women.

Data describing the gender wage gap are displayed in Figure 3.1. As shown, the gap changed little between 1960 and 1980, even as women entered the paid labor force in higher numbers. Over this period among full-time workers, women's median annual earnings as a percentage of men's remained flat at 60 percent. After 1980, however, the gap began to narrow. Women's earnings as a percent of men's rose rapidly in the 1980s, reaching 72 percent in 1990, then rising more gradually thereafter, reaching 83 percent in 2020 (US Census Bureau, 2020f).

Much of the increase after 1980 was due to women's increased work experience, greater remunerative returns to this experience, and greater representation in higher-paying professional and managerial occupations (Goldin, 2006: 22). However, even with this shift, a gap of 17 percentage points was still present as of 2020. Similar inequalities have been revealed in other domains as well, including the fact that in 2018 only twenty-four women were Chief Executive Officers (CEOs) of Fortune 500 companies (Zarya, 2018). Notably, the narrowing of the gender earnings gap occurred not only because women's earnings increased, but also because men's earnings declined (Bernhardt et al., 1995; Iceland and Redstone, 2020).

From a Social Justice perspective, these facts indicate that, despite recent advances, women still do not have the same chances for economic success as men. If they did, the logic goes, there would be no wage gap and half of all CEOs would be women. In short, because the Social Justice perspective tends to measure fairness in terms of equal outcomes, the fact that a wage gap exists at all and that women continue to be under-represented among CEOs provides clear evidence that economic and professional inequality continues to be unfairly imposed on women.

In contrast, the Social Order perspective argues that the overall gender pay gap is a poor indicator of discrimination against women because it fails to account for other factors that may produce such unequal outcomes. Such factors include the different choices men and women tend to make regarding college majors and fields of study and the characteristics of the occupations they find themselves in as a result. From the Social Order perspective, therefore, inequality among women and men in economic and professional outcomes does not, by itself, provide evidence of discrimination against women.

From a Social Order perspective, a major reason why the gender wage gap decreased in recent decades is that, during this time, women began completing college at

higher rates and selecting fields of study that better prepared them for more lucrative careers. For example,
throughout much of the twentieth century, women were
concentrated in a relatively small number of majors such
as education, literature, languages, and home economics
(Goldin, 2006). However, the number of women major-
ing in traditionally male-dominated fields, including
business, marketing, and accounting, increased rapidly
especially in the 1970s and 1980s. Now, women have
reached parity in these majors (Mann and DiPrete,
2013). In fact, today, women comprise the majority of
matriculants in medical and law schools (Association of
American Medical Colleges, 2017; Ward, 2016). And
since the early 1990s, women have been considerably
*more* likely to complete college than men. In 2020, 35
percent of men and 44 percent of women aged 25 to 29
had completed four or more years of college (US Census
Bureau, 2020b). This trend is illustrated in Figure 3.2.

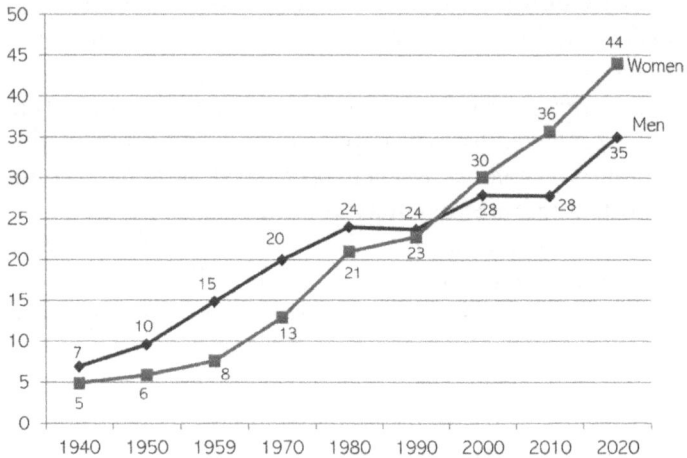

**Figure 3.2**   Percentage of 25- to 29-year-olds who have
completed four years of college or more, 1940–2020

*Source:* Data from US Census Bureau, 2020b

Nevertheless, women remain under-represented in certain science, technology, engineering, and mathematics (STEM) majors, such as computer science, physics, and electrical engineering (England and Li, 2006), while remaining over-represented in others. In 2017, 80 percent of Bachelor's degrees in Education and 78 percent of those in Psychology were awarded to women (Perry, 2018). If the earnings among STEM and education majors were similar, differences in the choice of major would have little bearing on the gender wage gap. But, of course, this is not the case. From a Social Order perspective, these sorting differences are important because they suggest that some part of the gender pay gap is due to the different choices that women and men make. This makes it difficult to interpret gender disparities as being solely due to discrimination.

Indeed, the choice of major strongly influences the type of job a student obtains after college. As noted earlier, in the early twentieth century, women were concentrated in occupations such as secretaries, clerks, and teachers. Even as late as 1970, about 65 percent of college-educated women were concentrated in a handful of occupations, including teachers, nurses, librarians, social or religious workers, and secretaries and other clerical workers. Gender differences began to decline thereafter, mainly as women moved into what had been predominantly "male" jobs, reflecting the decline in differences in college majors (Goldin, 2006).

Despite these declines in gender differences, many occupations remain disproportionately male or female. Today, women comprise about four-fifths of all schoolteachers and social workers, but just over a third of computer systems analysts, and about one in seven of architects and engineers. These patterns for 2016 are illustrated in Figure 3.3. There are also gender differences in jobs that do not require a high level of education; for

51

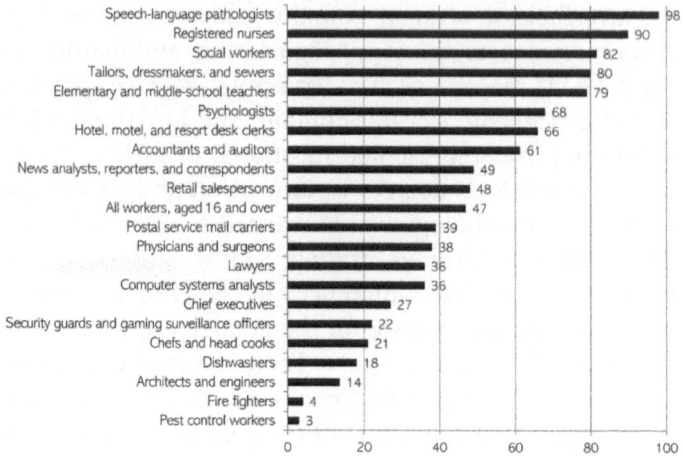

**Figure 3.3** Women as a percent of total employed in selected occupations, 2016

*Source:* Data from US Bureau of Labor Statistics, 2017

example, 22 percent of security guards are women, as are 4 percent of firefighters and 3 percent of pest control workers. It's worth noting that the gender composition of some of the occupations in Figure 3.3 has been changing rapidly. For example, in the five-year period between 2011 and 2016, the percentage of female physicians and surgeons increased from 34 percent to 38 percent, and for lawyers the increase was from 32 to 36 percent (US Bureau of Labor Statistics, 2012, 2017).

Overall, studies suggest that a significant proportion of the gender wage gap can be explained by factors other than discrimination – including differences in occupations, previous work experience, and the number of hours worked. The adjusted gender wage gap after these factors are taken into account is estimated to be somewhere between 5 to 8 percentage points, down from the unadjusted gap of close to 20 percent (Blau and Kahn, 2017; US Department of Labor, 2009).

Those from a Social Order perspective take these results to indicate that complaints about gender discrimination are exaggerated.

Of particular importance to the Social Order perspective is the "motherhood gap." This refers to the fact that women workers often choose to devote more of their time to child-rearing than men, and opt to work in lower wage, "family-friendly" occupations and industries. These jobs often provide relatively greater non-wage benefits, such as parental leave, sick leave, and a flexible schedule (Juhn and McCue, 2017; US Department of Labor, 2009). These include jobs such as elementary school teachers, home care aids, and real estate agents (Gendadek and West, 2011). Notably, one study found little difference in the wages of unmarried men and women aged 25 to 29 without children (Iceland and Redstone, 2020). Deciding to have children and orienting one's work life to facilitate caring for them thus plays a particularly important role in explaining the wage gap between women and men. Further supporting this notion, Figure 3.4 shows differences in labor force participation rates of parents by gender and age of children (US Department of Labor, 2020). Fathers with children under age 18 are much more likely to participate in the labor force (92 percent) than comparable mothers (71 percent); the difference is even starker among parents with children under 3 years old. In contrast, for the total population age 25 to 54, including those with and without children, the gap in labor force participation by gender is smaller than both gender gaps shown in Figure 3.4, with 88 percent of men in the labor force compared with 75 percent of women (US Bureau of Labor Statistics, 2021).

In short, those from the Social Order perspective highlight the small pay gap that remains after accounting for differences in other factors that predict wages.

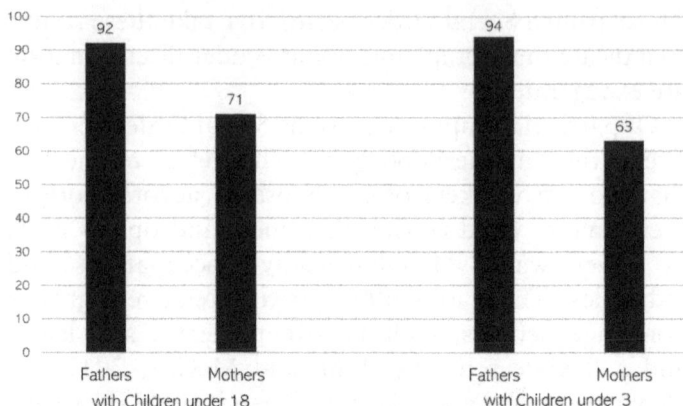

**Figure 3.4**   Labor force participation rates among parents by gender and age of children, 2020

*Source:* Data from US Department of Labor, 2020

To the Social Order observer, this indicates that we are approaching parity in access to professional opportunities, the main signifier of a fair process. In this view, fairness is achieved when equally qualified men and women have the same opportunities to be hired and are paid the same rate for the same work and not by whether they achieve equal representation in particular work sectors or positions.

In contrast, the Social Justice perspective views the narrowing of the wage gap after accounting for such factors as telling us little about working conditions and opportunities for women. The view is that the vestiges of patriarchal work structures and socialization processes, along with continued discrimination in the labor market, create and perpetuate gender roles that systematically disadvantage women. Because the Social Justice perspective views unequal outcomes as evidence of an unfair process, they favor policies that would equalize outcomes between women and men. If the elimination of discrimination in hiring and pay were as far as the efforts went, there would likely be little disagreement with those from a Social Order perspective. After all, eliminating discrimination is necessary for a fair process that offers equal opportunity to both women and men.

However, differences emerge because many with a Social Justice perspective would go further in their effort to equalize outcomes. Their efforts have included offering scholarships for women in majors in which they are under-represented, such as STEM. They might also include efforts to preferentially hire women in companies and occupations where they are under-represented (Shemla and Post, 2015). Companies such as Twitter and Pinterest, for example, launched programs in the 2010s to hire more women.

Other efforts attempt to change cultural practices and norms that are thought to socialize girls and boys into the pursuit of different interests and roles as adults. Some advocate teaching boys to be more nurturing and to foster compassion and appreciation for raising children (Minkel, 2018). Many also advocate for programs that get girls interested in STEM at an early age, for example by introducing girls to games that emphasize engineering principles, such as tool sets, blocks, and Legos (Johnson and Vega, 2019). In this way, the Social Justice approach moves beyond policies that ensure non-discrimination in job selection and promotion processes to those that actively promote equal outcomes by attempting to funnel more women into traditionally male-dominated jobs and professions and weaken traditional gender roles more generally.

Some people with a Social Order perspective may view the unequal provision of resources to girls and women as unfair to boys and men, who would then face systematic disadvantages in achieving their own educational or occupational goals. They might see the allocation of additional resources to women and girls as an inefficient and misplaced use of scarce goods. What is the point, they might ask, in trying to draw girls and women into educational and professional pursuits in which they might have relatively little interest?

## Freedom, Choice, and Responsibility

As already noted, the Social Order perspective tends to view freedom in terms of *options and opportunities*, while the Social Justice perspective tends to view freedom in terms of *power and influence*. With regards to gender inequality in the labor market, then, the Social Order perspective foregrounds two questions. This first is whether women have the opportunity to enter any profession they'd like. The second is whether, within their chosen profession, they have the opportunity to work to achieve upward mobility and earnings comparable to men. A common assertion here is that, while there may still be some discrimination in the workplace, women by-and-large have achieved equality of opportunity. As American Enterprise Institute scholar Mark Perry asserts:

> It's an important, but overlooked point that there really is no gender wage gap, rather, there's a gender earnings gap and that pay gap has almost nothing to do with gender discrimination. That is, there is almost no evidence that men and women working in the same position with the same background, education and qualifications are paid differently . . . To close the gender earnings gap, women . . . have to be willing to work more hours per week, more weeks per year, work more in higher-risk jobs and be more exposed to occupational injuries and fatalities (e.g., be willing to experience 50% of workplace fatalities instead of the current 7%), work

more in jobs that are physically demanding in more hostile work environments, be willing to commute longer distances, take less time off work for family reasons, take fewer sick days, be willing to accept higher-risk variable incomes like commission-based compensation, be willing to travel more and relocate more often, accept jobs with less human contact, sacrifice job-related personal fulfilment, etc. (Perry, 2017).

Thus, according to Perry, to close the remaining earnings gap between women and men, women will need to make choices that are similar to those of men. However, if women's tastes and preferences continue to differ from men's, women and men will continue to make different choices, which will continue to drive the earnings differential between them. Recall that freedom of choice, from the Social Order perspective, implies personal responsibility for one's outcomes; the individual is viewed as the responsible agent. In this sense, inequality and fairness are not necessarily at odds if the inequality results from people's freedom to make different choices.

In contrast, the Social Justice perspective points to differential socialization and gender discrimination that inhibit the freedom of women to achieve success. Because of these deeper societal forces, variation in outcomes between men and women must be a function of factors outside of either's control. The reality, however, is that in any hiring decision, the reasons for an adverse outcome may be difficult to discern. Therefore, when the affected person is female, her gender can always come into in play as a possible reason. That reason might be something as overt as actual hiring discrimination or as subtle as men using their male-dominated social networks to compete for jobs.

In short, while proponents of the Social Order perspective tend to believe that Social Justice proponents wrongly ignore the role of individual preferences and choices in shaping earnings differentials, proponents of the Social Justice perspective tend to believe that Social Order proponents wrongly ignore factors outside the individual's control in shaping such unequal outcomes.

The Social Justice perspective also sees social structures as inhibiting women's choices by tacitly encouraging them to be nurturing and expecting them to be primary caregivers within families. Conversely, the thinking goes, too little is done to socialize men into caregiving roles. Proponents of this perspective thus hold that progress in achieving gender equality has slowed in part because there has been slow progress toward changing this differential socialization process (Scarborough et al., 2019). Social psychologists Campbell Leaper and Carly Friedman have described the problem as follows: "As children develop, their gender self-concepts, beliefs, and motives are informed and transformed by families, peers, the media, and schools. These social contexts both reflect and perpetuate gender roles and gender inequities in the larger society" (Leaper and Friedman, 2007: 561).

In a similar vein, an additional, related point of contention between the two perspectives is the *source* of the differences between men and women. The Social Justice perspective assumes that men and women are similar at birth with respect to their talents and preferences, and that socialization largely explains the differences in the choices men and women make with regards to college majors, occupations, and family-work decisions. This assertion of sameness is sometimes referred to as a "blank slate" argument that sees environmental influences as much more important than innate ones in accounting for differences between the sexes. If all differences are socially generated, then, the thinking goes, we should be able to create social interventions to *undo* them. As a blog post published by the American Psychological Association argues:

> Media depictions of men and women as fundamentally "different" appear to perpetuate misconceptions – despite the lack of evidence. The resulting "urban legends" of gender difference can affect men and women at work and at home, as parents and as partners. As an example, workplace studies show that women who go against the caring, nurturing feminine stereotype may pay dearly for it when being hired or evaluated. And when it comes to personal relationships, best-selling books and popular magazines often claim that women and men don't get along because they communicate too differently. [Psychologist Janet Shibley] Hyde suggests instead that men and women stop talking prematurely because they have been led to believe that they can't change supposedly "innate" sex-based traits. (American Psychological Association, 2005)

In contrast, the Social Order perspective is more apt to consider that sex differences in tastes may have biological and evolutionary roots. Phyllis Schlafly, a noted conservative who fought against the passage of the Equal Rights Amendment in the 1970s, articulated this view in a 2014 interview on National Public Radio:

> A lot of people don't understand what feminism is. They think it is about advancement and success for women, but it's not that at all. It is about power for the female left. And they have this, I think, ridiculous idea that American women are oppressed by the patriarchy and we need laws and government to solve our problems for us . . . And they're always crying around about things like the differences between men and women are just a social construct. So they're really in a fight with human nature. (National Public Radio, 2014)

The idea that biological factors can play a role in differences between men and women is alarming from a Social Justice perspective. After all, attributing differences in outcomes between men and women to biology has previously been used to validate and justify existing inequalities. For example, in the past, some argued that the reason women were under-represented as managers was because they lack the aggressiveness and leadership ability often required to succeed in such positions (Terborg et al., 1977). From a Social Order perspective, however, it is dangerous to dismiss or avoid pursuing knowledge about possible innate differences between men and women simply because such differences may be used to justify inequality. This is why psychologist Steven Pinker has argued:

> There is, in fact, no incompatibility between the principles of feminism and the possibility that men and women are not psychologically identical. To repeat: equality is not the empirical claim that all groups of humans are interchangeable; it is the moral principle that individuals should not be judged or constrained by the average properties of their group . . . If we recognize this principle, no one has to spin myths about the indistinguishability of the sexes to justify equality. Nor should anyone invoke sex differences to justify discriminatory policies or to hector women into doing what they don't want to do. (Pinker, 2016: 340)

Empirical evidence on gender differences suggests that men are innately more interested in objects, and are thus more likely to become, for instance, engineers, while women are innately more interested in people, making them more likely to become, for instance, teachers (Lippa, 2010). Most Social Order advocates are quick to distinguish this point from a claim that biology is deterministic, as there are men who are more interested in people than the average woman, and women who are more interested in objects than the average man. A more accurate description of the assertion is that the differences, if real, may contribute to an unequal sorting, even in the absence of any gender socialization or discrimination.

The Social Order argument about preferences thus offers a particular, if partial, explanation for the lower representation of women in STEM fields. It emphasizes research showing a "gender equality paradox," whereby countries with more gender equality have *more* occupational segregation and fewer female graduates in STEM (Charles and Grusky, 2005; Stoet and Geary, 2018). Women in countries with low gender equality such as Albania and Algeria, for example, are more likely to major in STEM fields than women in more egalitarian countries like Norway and Sweden. Why? One possibility raised by researchers is that the opportunity costs of adhering to conventional gender roles is lower in higher income countries, allowing individuals in those contexts to select occupations with less concern about making ends meet compared to lower-income countries with weaker social safety nets (Charles and Grusky, 2005; Stoet and Geary, 2018). It's worth noting that there's no incompatibility between this assertion and a recognition that other reasons also contribute to women not entering some STEM fields, including a lack of female role models, gender stereotyping, and less family-friendly flexibility.

Returning to the goal of this book, how we think about the sources of these gender differences matters. Consider the following question: If we could snap our fingers and eliminate all gender discrimination and constraining aspects of socialization, would we expect a 50/50 distribution of men and women in every occupation?

In short, when it comes to understanding gender inequality across occupations, there is empirical support for the claim that both gender socialization and innate differences between women and men matter. The precise role that each plays, however, remains unknown, leaving a considerable amount of room for people's moral intuitions to drive their perceptions of the facts.

## *Individual and Group-Based Morality*

A person with a Social Justice orientation is likely to have moral intuitions that focus heavily on *caring for others*. Such a person is often particularly attuned to the plight of the vulnerable and oppressed. In contrast, a person with a Social Order orientation is likely to balance care for others with a concern for the social order, including the stability and cohesion of social groups. The implication of holding a Social Justice perspective toward gender inequality is as follows: gender discrimination and socialization must be vigorously opposed because they are oppressive – they reduce opportunities for girls and women and thus undermine their well-being.

A person with a Social Order orientation tends to be concerned not only with the well-being of women, but also with the impact of rapid social change on the well-being of families, communities, and society as a whole. As anthropologist Susan Harding wrote in 1981 about the debate between feminist and anti-feminist women: "the conflict among women over feminist reforms is rooted in competing ideological perspectives on the family. To summarize my argument briefly: At least since World War II, two prevalent ideologies of American family life can be discerned, one stressing ideas of equality, individualism, and reason, and the other stressing ideas of hierarchy, wholism, and morality" (Harding, 1981: 58).

The two groups described by Harding map well on to the individual and group-oriented moralities of the

Social Justice and Social Order perspectives, respectively. One of the reasons Phyllis Schlafly spoke so vociferously against feminism is because of her concern that feminism undermined the traditional family, a development she saw as socially destructive (Erwin, 2012). Similarly, those with a Social Order perspective are more likely to be concerned with potential tradeoffs between fulfilling the desires of individuals and serving the needs of the groups and institutions to which they belong.

To summarize, those whose moral intuitions promote Social Justice concerns will be more receptive to the idea that discriminatory structures produce unequal outcomes between men and women. In this line of thinking, injustice can and must be combatted through social interventions that reduce inequality. In contrast, those whose moral intuitions promote a concern with Social Order are more likely to regard existing social conventions regarding gender as serving a complex social purpose. They worry not only about individual outcomes, such as personal happiness, but also about maintaining adequate levels of group order and cohesion. They recognize that social conventions are prone to change as material conditions change, but they favor a gradual, organic shift that avoids destabilizing the society. If policy interventions are needed to effect such change, they prefer that such policies be implemented in a slow, deliberate, and incremental manner.

## Social Change

We have already alluded to the various approaches to social change favored by those with different moral intuitions in the contemporary American context. As described in the previous chapter, these differences are a function of three interrelated factors: (1) trust in the accumulated knowledge of evolved cultural systems versus trust in the ability of humankind to reengineer cultural systems to achieve desired ends; (2) the desire for sweeping versus incremental social change; and (3) a willingness to tolerate undesirable means to achieve desired ends.

The Social Justice perspective sees oppressive structures as responsible for producing unequal outcomes between men and women. Such injustice can and must be combatted through social interventions that reduce the gender gap, as exemplified by the various waves of feminist activity described above.

Because the focal moral concern of the Social Justice perspective is to protect the vulnerable, little weight is given to the potential negative effects of progressive changes on social institutions and social cohesion. For example, the rising divorce rate in the 1970s and the continued decline of the nuclear family headed by two parents may have been seen as unavoidable collateral damage – or perhaps even as necessary and thus a positive development – on the way to instituting gender equality. In any case, in the Social Justice view, problems that might arise from this kind of social change can be fixed by policy. For instance, government programs can be designed to support those who in a previous age may have remained married, or, if they divorced, relied on friends and family for support. These programs include welfare for single-parent families with children, tax breaks for families with children, and expanded daycare for the children of working parents, among many other federal and state programs that form our current safety net or have been discussed in recent policy debates.

In contrast, the Social Order perspective tends to be wary of rapid change that it sees as potentially destabilizing. It recognizes that social conventions are prone to change over time, but favors gradual changes that arise organically rather than rapid changes legislated by government agencies. Those who hold a Social Order perspective are particularly concerned with unintended consequences of social policies designed to equalize outcomes among individuals. Among the policies mentioned above, there is a concern that support provided by a governmental bureaucracy can never be as efficient as support provided by families and local communities. There is also a belief that support from local communities is better at fostering a sense of mutual responsibility than is government support. The sense of mutual responsibility means that, in addition to receiving benefits from one's community, people are expected to act responsibly, and when possible, reciprocate, to promote the greater good.

In the absence of this mutual understanding of rights and responsibilities, those with a Social Order perspective are inclined to worry about people gaming the system by taking more than they are entitled to and about people becoming dependent on government programs instead of working to become self-supporting. They argue, for example, that reliance on public assistance has a negative long-term effect on both those who receive aid and on society as a whole because it reduces incentives to work and self-sufficiency.

To summarize, those with a Social Justice orientation believe that waiting for gradual change toward a desired end is often futile and, to the extent that the suffering of vulnerable victims is at stake, morally reprehensible. They worry that those with an interest in maintaining the status quo will use their power to prevent needed changes from occurring, even as the call for change becomes more widespread. In contrast, individuals with a Social Order perspective recognize that social structures sometimes need to evolve, but worry that rapid change may "throw out the baby with the bathwater" by needlessly discarding the functioning elements of the current system.

## *Conclusion*

The issue of gender inequality is complex largely due to the difficulty of disentangling the role of systemic discrimination from the role of preferences and choices that sort men and women into different educational and occupational fields. Thus, even if there were no competing perspectives to navigate, adjudicating among the proposed causes of gender inequality in the United States would be no easy task. Gender discrimination – the cause given the most weight by those with a Social Justice perspective – is difficult to observe and measure. And depending on which other possible causes are taken into account, the magnitude of discrimination's effects diminish greatly. Preferences and choices – the causes given the most weight by those from the Social Order perspective – are also difficult to measure and therefore distinguish from other possible causes, particularly when one acknowledges that preferences and choices may themselves arise from exposure to patriarchal gender socialization.

We are thus left at an impasse from which data alone cannot, as of yet, free us. And as long as the Social Justice and Social Order perspectives continue to vie for dominion over the gender inequality narrative, progress toward understanding the nature of gender inequality in society will remain haltingly slow. Navigating the impasse will only become possible when we recognize and take seriously the different assumptions regarding fairness and equality; freedom, choice, and responsibility; individual and group-based morality; and attitudes toward social change by means of which those with a Social Justice and Social Order perspective tend to gather, view, and draw conclusions from data.

The divide between the two perspectives plagues our understanding of all forms of inequality, not just gender inequality. In the next chapter, we examine the role of the Social Justice and Social Order perspectives in shaping current debates about racial inequality.

# 4

# Racial Inequality

On some aspects of the subject of racial inequality there is broad agreement. For instance, most Americans believe that racial discrimination is unacceptable and that it continues to negatively affect many people of color (Horowitz et al., 2019). Yet, racial inequality is one of the most fiercely debated social problems in the United States today. Key points of contention include the extent to which discrimination is the *primary* driver of racial inequality and the types of remedies that would be both *fair* and *effective* in reducing such inequality. In this chapter, we show how the Social Justice–Social Order framework can help us understand these points of contention.

Those with a Social Justice perspective typically view discrimination as the primary, or sometimes only, driver of racial inequality. They often favor solutions, such as affirmative action, that seek to overcome discrimination by pressing for equal outcomes across groups. This view has gained considerable traction in recent years in many institutions, including universities, large corporations, and the mainstream press.

One of the indicators of the ascendance of the Social Justice perspective is a shift in the terminology used to refer to racial inequality. A content analysis of *The*

*New York Times*, for example, found steep increases in the 2010s in the salience of terms associated with this discrimination-centered view, including "Diversity and Inclusion," "Whiteness," "White Privilege," "Discrimination," "Social Justice," and "Systemic Racism" (Goldberg, 2019). "Anti-racism" also entered the lexicon, where an anti-racist policy has been defined as "any measure that sustains racial equity between racial groups" (Kendi, 2019a). The anti-racism movement is a particular manifestation of the Social Justice perspective with its near-exclusive focus on increasing the representation of groups seen as marginalized. For instance, Brown University's $100 million anti-racism plan, launched in 2015, sought to double the number of minority (and female) faculty and to devote resources to programs and centers specifically for students and faculty of marginalized groups (McCammond, 2015). Countless other colleges and universities have launched similar – though less well-funded – initiatives.

In contrast, those with a Social Order perspective are skeptical of the current emphasis on discrimination as the sole or main cause of inequality. For example, they are more likely to point out the heterogeneity of outcomes within racial groups and to highlight the importance of class background and/or culture in shaping how individuals fare today (Hughes, 2018; Murray, 2012). They view approaches to reducing inequality that focus only on reducing discrimination as problematic and ultimately unhelpful. As they see it, such approaches do not take a comprehensive view of the sources of racial disparities.

One advocate of this latter perspective is the economist Glenn Loury. He writes:

> I am not a big fan of the structural racism narrative.
> I think it is imprecise; I think that those who invoke

structural racism are begging the question. I want to know exactly what structures, what dynamic processes, they mean, and I want to know exactly how race figures into that story ... I am offering instead, as a counterpoint to the bias narrative, what I am calling the development narrative, which stresses that patterns of behavior within the disadvantaged population need to be looked at. (Loury, 2020)

Later in the same article, Loury points to lower educational outcomes and the prevalence of single-parent families among African Americans as factors contributing to inequality. In his view, advocating for affirmative action, reparations, or quotas to reduce disparities makes little sense because they leave the root causes of inequality untouched. Loury instead argues that improving and equalizing educational *opportunities* would be a more effective long-term solution.

In the rest of this chapter, we look at how people's views on racial inequality are shaped by whether they approach the issue from a Social Justice or a Social Order perspective. We highlight how debates over this issue hinge on different views about the causes of racial inequality today and how best to address it.

## *Social Order and Social Justice*

The tension between the Social Order and Social Justice perspectives has been present from the founding of the nation. The American emphasis on the importance of equality – a central feature of the Social Justice perspective – has deep roots. The most often quoted sentence from the Declaration of Independence asserts that, "We hold these truths to be self-evident, that all men are created equal, that they are endowed by their

Creator with certain unalienable Rights, that among these are Life, Liberty and the pursuit of Happiness." To many, this declaration represents a revolutionary mission statement. Written during a time of violence, despotism, slavery, and cruelty, it laid out a vision for the equal treatment of individuals under the law. It was a pledge to a new kind of Social Justice.

Others have highlighted the limitations, and even hypocrisy, of the Declaration. After all, at the time it was written and for many years to come, it applied primarily or exclusively to white men of means. In many states, men could not vote if they didn't own property, and women and nonwhites could not vote at all (Free, 2015). Concerns about disrupting the social order of the day were prominent in debates regarding what to do about the institution of slavery (Helo and Onuf, 2003). This was settled only with the Civil War and the ratification of the 13th Amendment in 1865, which finally abolished slavery in the United States.

Even then we saw the persistence of white supremacy when, beginning in the 1870s, many Southern states adopted "Jim Crow" laws. These laws essentially mandated segregation in public places such as buses and trains, and banned blacks from white hotels, barber shops, restaurants, and theaters (Christian and Bennett, 1998: 282; Franklin and Moss, 2000: 290). By the middle decades of the twentieth century, however, the Social Justice perspective surged, culminating in the Civil Rights movement. Perhaps the crowning achievement of this movement was the passage of the Civil Rights Act of 1964, which outlawed discrimination based on race, color, religion, sex, and national origin, and was applied to voter registration requirements, schools, employment, and public accommodations.

In Chapter 2, we argued that the Social Justice and Social Order perspectives each emphasize different beliefs and intuitions concerning: fairness and equality; freedom, choice, and responsibility; individual and group-based morality; and attitudes toward social change. We now discuss each of these in turn with respect to racial inequality in America today.

## *Fairness and Equality*

The Social Justice perspective tends to measure fairness by the degree to which outcomes are proportional across groups. This means that racial inequality, including gaps in education, income, and health, is seen as evidence of an unfair system, often described as the result of structural racism, systemic racism, or white supremacy. According to this perspective, the current social system supports discrimination in labor and housing markets, unequal treatment in the criminal justice system, and underinvestment in schools in minority neighborhoods, among other unequal practices and policies. And the inequalities that persist in these domains are seen as evidence of racial discrimination.

Figures 4.1–4.3 show trends over the past several decades in common indicators of socioeconomic status: education, poverty, and income (US Census Bureau, 2020b, 2020a, 2020e). They reveal large differences between whites on the one hand and blacks and Hispanics on the other across all three measures. In 2020, among adults 25 years and older, 38 percent of whites had completed four or more years of college compared to 28 percent of blacks and 21 percent of Hispanics. Median household income exhibited a similar pattern. For whites in 2020, the median income was $71,231, compared to $55,321 for Hispanics and $45,870 for blacks. Similar disparities are reflected in poverty rates across groups, as shown in Figure 4.2.

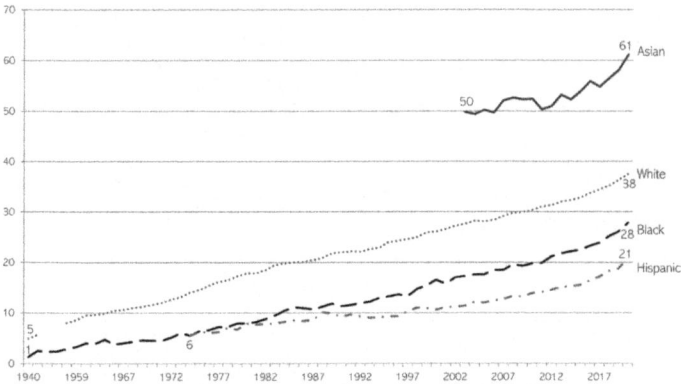

**Figure 4.1**   Percent of people 25 years and older who have completed college, by race and ethnicity, 1940–2020

*Note:* The figures for whites, blacks, and Asians are for all people who identify as those groups regardless of Hispanic origin. This modestly affects overall percentages. For example, in 2020, 38 percent of all whites completed college, compared to 42 percent of non-Hispanic whites.

*Source:* Data from US Census Bureau, 2020b

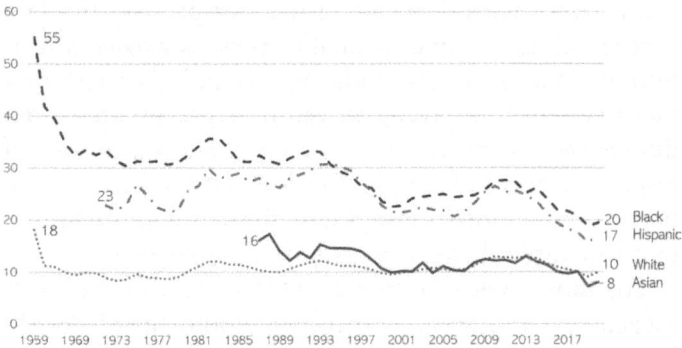

**Figure 4.2**   Percent poor, by race and ethnicity, 1959–2020

*Note:* The figures for whites, blacks, and Asians are for all people who identify as those groups regardless of Hispanic origin. This moderately affects overall percentages. For example, the poverty rate of all whites in 2020 was 10.1 percent, compared to 8.2 percent among non-Hispanic whites.

*Source:* Data from US Census Bureau, 2020a

73

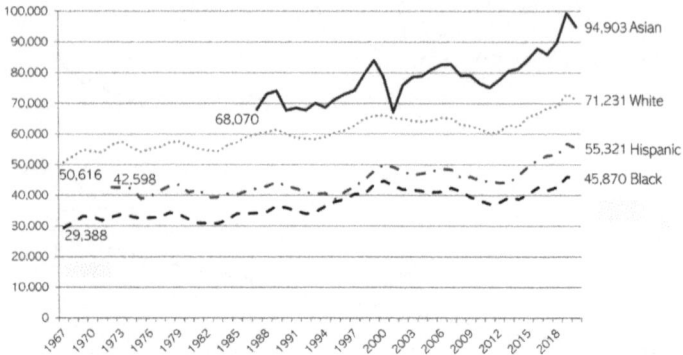

**Figure 4.3**   Median household income (constant 2020 dollars), by race and ethnicity, 1967–2020

*Note:* The figures for whites, blacks, and Asians are for all people who identify as those groups regardless of Hispanic origin. This modestly affects overall median incomes. For example, the median income for all whites was $71,231 in 2020, compared to $74,912 for non-Hispanic whites.

*Source:* Data from US Census Bureau, 2020e

For those with a Social Justice perspective, the fact that racial and ethnic inequality persists across education, income, and other indicators is an indictment of a racist system that produced and now perpetuates those differences. In this line of thinking, there is a history of discrimination and marginalization that produced severe barriers for minority groups, and the forces and attitudes that generated those barriers haven't gone away.

To those with a Social Order perspective, this racism-centered story is incomplete and therefore less compelling. They might ask – if systemic racism is the sole or primary determining factor of inequality, how are Asians in the US doing so well, with education levels and incomes far surpassing those of other groups, including whites? Indeed, the figures show that the college completion rate and median household income among Asians was 61 percent and $94,903, respectively, in

2020, while the comparable figures for whites were just 38 percent and $71,231.

There is also considerable variability in outcomes within the broader pan-ethnic groups. This variation suggests that racism is not the primary, let alone the only, cause of racial inequality in the US. The implication is that we need to do a better job considering the role of social class in shaping how people do within racial and ethnic groups (Hughes, 2018; Murray, 2012). For instance, among Asian ethnic groups, those of Indian origin have much higher levels of education and income than the Hmong and Cambodians, who have median household incomes similar to those of whites. Among Hispanics, the highest socioeconomic outcomes are observed among Argentines and Chileans, who surpassed whites in terms of educational attainment and income. Among numerically large Hispanic groups, Cubans had the highest levels of income and education, though they lagged behind whites. Mexicans, by far the largest Hispanic group in the US, had a substantially higher poverty rate and significantly lower median income than those of whites (Iceland, 2017). These figures are illustrated in Table 4.1.

Other research has indicated that some black immigrant groups also fare well. For instance, second-generation Nigerian Americans have higher levels of education than native-born whites, and their wages are similar to whites even after taking into account many variables like age, education, and US region of residence (Sakamoto et al., 2021). Even among whites, outcomes differ considerably by ancestry. People of Russian descent have a substantially higher income than those of French descent (Hughes, 2018).

Returning to the theme of *fairness* and *equality*, if one takes the position that gaps in education, income, and poverty are sufficient evidence of systemic racism,

**Table 4.1**  Characteristics of selected ethnic groups, 2016

|  | % with college degree | % poor | Median household income ($) |
|---|---|---|---|
| White | 35 | 12 | 60,400 |
| Black | 24 | 23 | 38,000 |
| Asian | 56 | 12 | 79,800 |
| Chinese | 59 | 16 | 73,500 |
| Indian | 78 | 7 | 109,000 |
| Filipino | 54 | 6 | 88,900 |
| Vietnamese | 32 | 14 | 62,000 |
| Hmong | 19 | 21 | 61,600 |
| Cambodian | 20 | 15 | 59,000 |
| Hispanic | 17 | 21 | 46,300 |
| Mexican | 13 | 22 | 46,010 |
| Puerto Rican | 21 | 23 | 42,000 |
| Cuban | 30 | 17 | 45,800 |
| Salvadoran | 11 | 18 | 40,000 |
| Argentinian | 47 | 11 | 70,000 |
| Chilean | 45 | 11 | 68,600 |

*Note:* Educational attainment is for the population aged 25+.
*Source:* Analysis of American Community Survey (ACS) data

as many from the Social Justice perspective do, then the appropriate response is to reform the current system and introduce new policies to ensure a more equal, and thus fairer, outcome. This extends not only to education and income more generally, but also to representation in a wide variety of organizations as well as in positions of power and influence. As one author put it while discussing the increase in the diversity of Oscar nominees in 2021:

> Indeed, the fact that it took until 2021 for the Academy Awards to recognize a widely heterogeneous array of nominees also speaks directly to the deeply entrenched prejudices that have kept people of color outside of the Oscars – and the film industry at large – for so long.

"We're seeing notable gains for different communities, and it is important to celebrate that," says Dr. Stacy L. Smith, of USC's Annenberg Inclusion Initiative. "There are still voices missing – for example, [*One Night in Miami* director] Regina King was left out of the directing nominations and few if any Latinx nominees were named this year – so there is room for the Academy to continue its efforts. We will continue to watch the nominations to ensure that a year of 'firsts' does not become a year of 'only.'" (Vary, 2021)

Other advocates of the Social Justice perspective note that, while there might be less discrimination today, the legacy of inequality and persistent unfairness mean that affirmative action needs to continue until outcomes have been equalized. In an opinion piece in the *Kansas State Collegian*, a student author wrote:

Minorities with a history of discrimination and even outright oppression are notably less well-off. According to the US Census Bureau, the median income of black families was less than two-thirds that of the median of all US families in 2009. It is for this reason that affirmative action is necessary. In the past, discriminated minorities have been denied opportunities necessary for proper growth. Even though those opportunities are available to them now, they are at a disadvantage because they have to make up for lost time. In the end, this can and will balance itself out. As more opportunities become available, those who have been denied in the past will be increasingly better positioned to take advantage of them. In order to establish this happy medium and to make sure opportunities are not being unjustly withheld, affirmative action is necessary. (Hellmer, 2013)

Those from the Social Order perspective, in contrast, argue that, while discrimination still occurs, it does so much less than in the past, and therefore is no longer the primary driver of racial inequality. In this view, other factors, such as differences in behaviors across groups, human and social capital, and cultural values likely play a larger role today. Thus, according to the Social Order perspective, focusing on "systemic racism" and discriminatory practices will not address the root causes of the problem because most inequality is not due to either of those factors. After all, the high achievement observed among some minority groups, according to this perspective, couldn't happen in a system dominated by white supremacy.

From the Social Order perspective, a *fair* system needs to maintain selection processes that focus on the relevant qualifications and skills of the individual being considered – and not on their race. Doing so is seen as crucial for selecting he best talent and maintaining the legitimacy of the social order. Affirmative action policies that go beyond trying to attract a diverse group of qualified candidates by giving some candidates preferential treatment based on criteria unrelated to job performance are considered fundamentally unfair and threaten to undermine the social order. As writer and commentator Berlin Fang argues in *The Federalist*:

> AA [affirmative action] was originally created to provide equal opportunity for all qualified persons. It has been reduced nowadays to a mere vehicle towards greater diversity on superficial levels, at the sacrifice of other principles that make America a great nation, including equality and fairness for all. AA has evolved into a great irony in American life: To strengthen some groups' ability for social mobility, other groups have to yield, stop, or be run over. In college admissions, affirmative action practices have created reverse discrimination for white

Americans and blatant racism against Asian Americans. (Fang, 2019)

Other Social Order advocates further argue that affirmative action is an overly blunt tool that goes too far in equating race with disadvantage. They point to the diversity of backgrounds and experiences of individuals *within* racial groups. This type of criticism is exemplified by an opinion piece in *The Cornell Review* where the author writes:

> Unfortunately, the problem with racial-based affirmative action is that it is a system created by those who fail to understand demographic complexities and instead opt for conveniently-named race categories. The system of affirmative action categorizes applicants into convenient categories with disregard to the specific ethnic or socio-economic background of that individual. One of my roommates during high school was a beneficiary of the affirmative action system in the United States. He was a transfer from one of the most prominent British Public Schools in London, had several extremely expensive clothing items including a Rolex watch, and regularly took his meals by Ubering to luxury restaurants in the area. Yet as a Spanish citizen, he was a Hispanic and therefore received preference in college admissions over other applicants, and was the only applicant from my high school accepted early decision into his Ivy League university. Of course, this may be an extreme example, but it is not one rare anomaly. (Ahn, 2018)

In summary, a key point in the discussion of inequality and fairness is that those from the Social Justice perspective are much more likely to view existing inequalities between groups as the result of an *unfair* system. In contrast, those from the Social Order perspective are less likely to see fairness and inequality in opposition. A fair (evenly applied, merit-based) selection process may yield outcomes that are unequal on a number of dimensions, including sex, race, sexual orientation, and so on, provided the members of these groups on average exhibit differences in other factors that shape success. The Social Order perspective thus views inequality between groups as something that is not by definition problematic and that can happen for benign reasons that have nothing to do with systemic racism. In the following section, we shed further light on the two perspectives' disagreement over the causes of racial inequality as we discuss their different interpretations of freedom, choice, and responsibility.

### Freedom, Choice, and Responsibility

The Social Justice perspective understands freedom in terms of power and influence. The under-representation of minority group members in positions of power and influence is an indication of their oppression. According to this view, systemic racism blocks opportunities through policies that disproportionately and negatively affect people of color. The Social Justice response is that merely removing barriers is insufficient. The answer is to also apply policies that produce proportionate representation and, in turn, equalize power. It is only then that people will truly have the freedom to pursue their goals. As philosophy professor Susan Stark argues:

> [I]t is important to be up front about the use of race in the justification for affirmative action programs. If colleges fail to use race as an explicit factor in admissions, and fail to use race to rectify past and ongoing injustice, they will instead use race implicitly to deny admission to those who continue to experience racial oppression

and discrimination and will thus be complicit in racial oppression. (Stark, 2004: 216)

In contrast, the Social Order perspective sees freedom in terms of the ability to pursue opportunities for well-being and success within the larger system without restriction. A proponent of this perspective would not expect everyone to fare the same, as people vary in their talents, tastes, values, ambition, and effort. From this perspective, individuals are at least partly, if not largely, responsible for the outcomes they experience. Here, freedom is seen as the ability to succeed or fail based on one's merit and effort.

Many people who favor the Social Order perspective today would agree that barriers to opportunity, including racial discrimination, should be removed to the greatest extent possible. However, they also believe we should be wary of efforts to equalize outcomes, such as affirmative action. This is not only because such efforts are seen as unfair but because they restrict the freedom of qualified individuals who are not members of protected groups to pursue *their* goals. This, they argue, is the inevitable outcome of policies that reserve specific educational and employment opportunities for members of preferred groups.

While recognizing that racial bias has not been and in fact may never be completely eliminated from the hearts and minds of individuals, a person with a Social Order perspective nonetheless is receptive to the idea that racial discrimination has been reduced to the point where it cannot be blamed for all or even most current inequalities. As such, they may view efforts to further reduce discrimination as being of marginal value at best. They would argue instead that efforts should be directed toward strengthening community institutions, such as schools. Further efforts should be made to inculcate a sense of self-efficacy and responsibility among under-represented groups to give them the confidence and ability they need to flourish in a competitive system. In this vein, Jason Riley, a black conservative critic of affirmative action, argues that: "half a century after the civil rights battles were fought and won, liberalism remains much more interested in making excuses for blacks than in reevaluating efforts to help them." Elsewhere in his book he asserts that "black cultural attitudes toward work, authority, dress, sex and violence have also proven counterproductive, inhibiting the development of the kind of human capital that has led to socioeconomic advancement for other groups" (Riley, 2014: 174, 50).

In short, disagreement over the extent to which contemporary inequality is due to systemic racism versus personal factors over which individuals have control shapes much of the divergence between the Social Justice and Social Order perspectives.

What do the data tell us? Interpreting the evidence on this topic is complicated, and those from a Social Justice and Social Order perspective tend to do it differently.

### Critical Race Theory and Systemic Racism

The Social Justice perspective today is deeply influenced by a way of understanding the world that emphasizes the roles of structural racism and discrimination in sustaining racial inequality. This is often referred to as critical race theory. Critical race theory has its origins in multiple disciplines, including the broader umbrella of critical theory, which emerged among a group of sociologists at the University of Frankfurt in the 1930s.

Critical theory focused primarily on how power and domination operate in society. It is tied to the

82

development of postmodern theory, which highlights how people in general and elites in particular use language to shape discourse on social issues to maintain power. Critical race theory also draws from critical legal studies, a body of scholarship formulated in the 1970s, which holds that the law codifies society's biases against oppressed groups (Delgado and Stefancic, 2001).

Critical race theory aligns with the Social Justice perspective because it holds that systemic racism against members of marginalized groups, rather than the group members' individual behaviors or values, explains their relative disadvantage both historically and today. Examples of systemic racism include the steering of minority home seekers to minority neighborhoods in a way that maintains segregation; redlining (the widespread practice in the mid twentieth century of banks not providing home loans to people living in high-poverty and majority-black neighborhoods); the racial gerrymandering of voting districts as a strategy to dilute the voting power of minority group members; racial profiling and anti-minority violence by law enforcement; and informal discrimination against minority job seekers (Massey and Denton, 1993: 115–147). According to critical race theory, whites may be unaware of the privileges they receive due to their skin color, such as greater social status and the ability to move, work, and play more freely than others (McIntosh 2003). The fact that whites have, on average, higher levels of education, higher earnings, and are less likely to be incarcerated that many other groups is seen by those from the Social Justice perspective as evidence of continued systemic racism.

Critical race theory increasingly forms the foundation for how many people learn about race and racial relations in the US today. Its reach now extends from

K-12 schools and colleges to mainstream media and into much of popular culture. For example, in a blog on health disparities, Monique Tello, a practicing physician and clinical instructor at Harvard Medical School, discussing health disparities, provided the following anecdote about a patient who received poor care, and posited that it was due to the fact that she was black. Dr. Tello framed the situation squarely within the critical race theory perspective, arguing that:

> Cases like my patient's . . . illustrate the negative assumptions and associations we can label racism, but "most physicians are not explicitly racist and are committed to treating all patients equally. However, they operate in an inherently racist system." [(Hardeman et al., 2016)] In addition, we know that our own subconscious prejudices, also called implicit bias, can affect the way we treat patients . . . We now recognize that racism and discrimination are deeply ingrained in the social, political, and economic structures of our society. For minorities, these differences result in unequal access to quality education, healthy food, livable wages, and affordable housing. In the wake of multiple highly publicized events, the Black Lives Matter movement has gained momentum, and with it have come more strident calls to address this ingrained, or *structural*, racism, as well as implicit bias. (Tello, 2017; emphasis in the original)

More generally, substantial evidence indicates that discrimination against blacks in the labor market persists. Studies in which otherwise similar white and black candidates inquire about jobs ("audit studies") have shown that black job seekers are less likely to receive callbacks or job offers than whites (Quillian et al., 2017). Sociologist Devah Pager and her colleagues found that, in the low-wage market in New York City, when black and white applicants were matched on demographic characteristics and interpersonal skills, black applicants were half as likely as equally qualified white applicants to receive a callback or job offer (Pager et al., 2009). Similar studies have documented discrimination in housing searches (Ross and Turner, 2005) and home mortgage applications (Turner and Skidmore, 1999), although discrimination in housing has declined over time (Ross and Turner, 2005).

While audit studies demonstrate the role of contemporary discrimination, the *legacy of past discrimination* shapes current outcomes as well. This means that, even if there were no discrimination today, inequality would persist because disadvantage has been transmitted across generations. For example, there is a positive overall correlation (it is about 0.32) between a parent and child's position in the income distribution (as measured by income quintile) and this has changed little over time (Chetty et al., 2014). Wealth is also transferred across generations via inheritance, so if the wealth of the previous generations was limited due to discrimination, that disadvantage would be passed down to the next generations.

The legacy of historical inequalities, especially regarding African Americans, has many components. One important component is high levels of residential segregation. Neighborhoods vary widely in the amenities they provide, ranging from the quality of local schools to levels of social disorganization, cohesion, and crime, to the presence of parks and recreational opportunities. To the extent that African Americans are concentrated in poor neighborhoods, racial residential segregation reduces their access to employment opportunities in other parts of the city, the amount of social capital they can acquire (in terms of social networks that lead to employment and mobility), and the provision of good schools, while increasing their exposure to poverty and its accompanying problems (Massey and Denton, 1993: 148–185).

Encouragingly, residential segregation has gradually declined over the past several decades. For example, in 1980 the typical African American lived in a neighborhood that was 61 percent black. By 2010 that figure had declined to 46 percent (Iceland and Sharp, 2013). However, neighborhoods generally change slowly, and segregation, while it has declined substantially, remains high in absolute terms, especially for African Americans. Thus, it is likely that differences in the types of neighborhoods people live in still matter for their future prospects (Sharkey, 2016).

Asians in the United States historically have experienced considerable discrimination, such as with the 1882 Chinese Exclusion Act that barred immigration from China. Few would claim that discrimination against Asians is a thing of the past, although discrimination, past or present, does not appear to substantially reduce their average socioeconomic achievement. Their wages are similar to those of native-born whites even after taking into account education, family structure, age, and other demographic characteristics (Wang et al., 2017).

In contrast, Latinos continue to fare worse in terms of income, wealth, and education than the native-born white population, despite their upward mobility across generations. The impact of discrimination itself on Latinos is unclear, though research suggests that it may be a significant obstacle for darker-skinned Latinos (Telles and Ortiz, 2008: 233–234).

Overall, the research on discrimination suggests that it has played a significant historical role in the development of racial socioeconomic inequalities in the US, particularly for African Americans and for some Hispanics. However, evidence regarding its role in maintaining current levels of inequality among race groups, as emphasized by the Social Justice perspective, is mixed, leaving room for other factors to be considered.

## Factors Other than Discrimination that Help Explain Racial and Ethnic Differences

The Social Justice perspective places most, if not all, of the blame for current inequality on current discrimination and systemic racism. In contrast, according to the Social Order perspective, while discrimination may play a role, other factors, including culture, human capital, and the immigrant incorporation process, need to be considered, and indeed are more important than contemporary discrimination for understanding patterns of inequality.

### Culture

Culture refers to the beliefs, values, customs, behaviors, and other characteristics that are shared and accepted by a group of people. Culture is not deterministic, in that people who share a culture do not always act in the same way when presented with a similar situation. Rather, culture defines the range of generally accepted beliefs and behaviors at one's disposal when considering a course of action.

Discussions of the effect of culture on poverty and racial inequality are fraught. Invoking culture as an explanatory factor is often interpreted as "blaming the victim" for their disadvantaged position, because culture highlights the role of values and choices in determining outcomes. Consider, for instance, the reaction to the 1965 report *The Negro Family: The Case for National Action*. The report was penned by sociologist Daniel Patrick Moynihan, who was then serving in the

Lyndon B. Johnson administration (Moynihan, 1965). The report described the "tangle of pathology" among black families in the US, noting that one-fourth of black babies were born to unmarried mothers. While Moynihan prefaced his discussion by noting the importance of historical and contemporary discrimination in producing inequality, he was attacked by a number of people as being patronizing and racist (Patterson, 2000: 100).

Regardless of where one stands on Moynihan's report, many advocates of the Social Order perspective see the questions it raised as relevant today. As a point of comparison, while in 1965 the fraction of births to unwed black mothers that worried Moynihan was about one-quarter, in 2017, 69 percent of black births were to unmarried women, as were 28 percent of white births, 52 percent of Hispanic births, and 12 percent of Asian births (Martin et al., 2018: 25). If Moynihan was correct, that the percentage in 1965 was cause for alarm, then the numbers today – even after allowing for the effect of shifting social norms on cohabitation – would be extremely concerning.

Family formation patterns are clearly tied to people's economic well-being. As shown in Figure 4.4., about 32 percent of female-headed families with children were poor in 2020, compared to just 6 percent of married-couple families with children (US Census Bureau, 2021a). These differences by family structure are large for every racial and ethnic group. For example, 6 percent and 8 percent of white and African American married couple families with children are poor, compared to 31 and 36 percent of white and African American single female-headed families with children. Single parents often struggle to earn sufficient income for their families while also having the time and energy to provide a nurturing environment for their children. Children raised

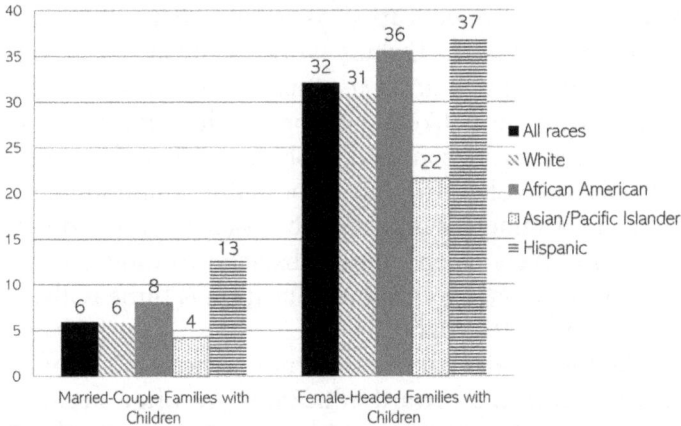

**Figure 4.4** Poverty rates by family structure, race, and Hispanic origin, 2020

*Source:* Data from US Census Bureau, 2021a

in single-parent households have lower average levels of educational attainment and a greater likelihood of social and emotional problems than children raised in intact married-couple families (McLanahan, 2004: 203).

Those with a Social Order perspective often argue that this difference is due, in part, to the difficulty single-headed households experience in instilling success-oriented values and behaviors in their children. Absent such values and behaviors, the children of single parents living in poor communities are more likely to succumb to a surrounding culture that promotes values and goals that contribute to economic failure (Murray, 2012; Sowell, 2005).

A related cultural mechanism that has been theorized as affecting levels of racial inequality – and differences in school performance in particular – is *oppositional culture*. This theory, as developed by the anthropologist John Ogbu, posits that a minority group's historical relationship to the dominant group plays a role in whether it views education as a method for advancement. According to Ogbu's work, members of groups who voluntarily migrate to a nation where they are a minority are more likely to embrace education as a way to achieve socioeconomic mobility. Whereas groups who were involuntarily incorporated in a nation where they are a minority (due to either slavery or conquest) are more likely to encounter obstacles to mobility and thus believe that investing in education is futile (Gibson and Ogbu, 1991; Ogbu, 1991).

The theory also asserts that those who don't adopt a negative attitude toward education are often accused, at least in the American context, of "acting white" (Downey, 2008; Fordham and Ogbu, 1986). This may lead young people to adopt a psychologically protective stance of embracing an identity that is in opposition to institutions dominated by the white majority (Ogbu, 1978, 2003). The focus on choice makes Ogbu's oppositional theory appealing to those with a Social Order perspective, while those with a Social Justice perspective often argue that these harmful cultural patterns are themselves traceable to racism. Either way, the question remains of what to do if, over time, oppositional culture becomes self-sustaining, independent of racism, and thus unresponsive to reductions in racism in society.

Ogbu noted that culture may also help explain *high* levels of education among some immigrant groups. For example, among Jews, the historic emphasis of rabbinic Judaism on the analysis of religious texts and the value placed on the knowledge of Jewish law strongly encouraged literacy and schooling for Jewish children. This value may have contributed to the ease with which Jews embraced education as a vehicle for upward mobility (Burstein, 2007).

Similarities have been pointed out among Asian groups. Sociologists Alejandro Portes and Ruben Rumbaut, in a study of second-generation Southeast Asian groups, noted that parents place heavy emphasis on homework and study (Portes and Rumbaut, 2001). Likewise, sociologists Amy Hsin and Yu Xie find that greater academic effort among Asian students is the most important factor explaining the Asian academic advantage over whites. They attribute this to a cultural emphasis on academic achievement that is also reflected in the investment of many Asian parents in supplemental schooling, private tutoring, and college preparation (Hsin and Xie, 2014).

Despite evidence suggesting that culture matters, the *magnitude* of its effect on racial inequality is nearly impossible to determine. First, culture is difficult to measure. Quantitative studies thus often rely on proxy measures, such as the prevalence of single-parent families, even though they may not be wholly the result of cultural forces.

Second, there is considerable debate about whether cultural practices are a *cause* or an *outcome* of inequality. Consider once again the example of differences in poverty across racial and ethnic groups and the role that family formation plays. It has been argued by those with a Social Order perspective that single-parenthood *causes* poverty because single-parent families have higher poverty rates than two-parent families. However, the causal order might also be the reverse: poverty and inequality may affect family-formation patterns.

Those with a Social Justice perspective are more likely to argue that the decline in job opportunities for low-skilled men due to deindustrialization and globalization is an important cause of declining marriage rates (Wilson, 1987). Since African American men are overrepresented in many low-skilled and blue-collar jobs, this may have impacted them more than members of other racial groups. The relatively low levels of employment of young black men also likely affects marriage rates. As sociologist William Julius Wilson has argued, "The black delay in marriage and the lower rate of remarriage, each associated with high percentages of out-of-wedlock births and female-headed households, can be directly tied to the employment status of black males" (Wilson, 1987).

The Social Order–Social Justice framework can help explain why people arrive at different conclusions regarding these complex issues. Those with a Social Justice perspective tend to emphasize that structural conditions determine culture. In highlighting structural conditions, responsibility (blame) for individual outcomes is placed on society rather than on individuals. According to this perspective, systemic racism constrains people of color, which causes them to underperform relative to other groups. In contrast, those from the Social Order perspective tend to emphasize that, while many people undoubtedly face constraints and obstacles, they none-theless have the ability to make responsible choices that can increase their upward mobility. In this line of thinking, cultural norms and values that lead to success-oriented individual decision-making must be cultivated if racial inequality is to be reduced.

Overall, the empirical evidence reviewed above indicates that culture may be an important factor that shapes human behavior and helps explain racial inequality. The extent of its explanatory power, however, continues to generate debate among those with the Social Justice and Social Order perspectives. Similar debates occur regarding the influence of human capital.

*Human capital*
Human capital refers to one's level of education and the skills learned through work experience. Earlier in this chapter, we showed that blacks and Hispanics have lower average levels of education than whites. In

contrast, Asians' average levels of educational attainment tend to be higher than whites. These patterns help explain why median household incomes and wages are highest among Asians, followed by whites, while those of Hispanics and blacks are considerably lower (Iceland, 2017; Sakamoto et al., 2009).

Because education is so highly correlated with income, those from the Social Order perspective emphasize the importance of individuals pursuing higher education as a means to achieve higher incomes. For instance, a 2018 research report focusing on Millennials by sociologists Wendy Wang and W. Bradford Wilcox asserts that financial well-being is much more likely if one follows the "success sequence," which entails graduating from high school, getting married, and having children – in that order. They find that over 90 percent of black, Hispanic, Asian, and white Millennials who follow this sequence avoid poverty in young adulthood (Wang and Wilcox, 2018).

Those from the Social Justice perspective agree that education is important, but they are more likely to emphasize that society is structured in a way that prevents certain racial groups from seeking out and acquiring a good education. Blacks and Hispanics living in segregated neighborhoods are more likely to attend low-performing schools, which in turn reduces their probability of attending college. In this way, according to the Social Justice perspective, social structure once again constrains the freedom of individuals to make choices that would enhance their future well-being (Massey and Denton, 1993: 141–142).

*Immigrant assimilation*

To fully understand patterns and trends in the well-being of Hispanics and Asians in particular – the two fastest growing racial/ethnic groups in the United States

– one must take into account the fact that a significant proportion of each group was born outside of the US. As of 2019, nearly a third of Hispanics and two thirds of Asians in the United States were born abroad (US Census Bureau, 2021b, 2021c). Newcomers may not have incomes on par with those of the native-born population if they are younger, come with low levels of education, do not speak English well, or lack access to the full range of jobs available in the labor market due to their citizenship or visa status. For these reasons, what matters more for understanding the patterns of well-being is the socioeconomic attainment of their children and subsequent generations.

Overall, the evidence supports the prediction made by assimilation theory that subsequent generations will fare better than the foreign-born generation. Bearing this out, native-born Asians and Hispanics tend to have better outcomes than the foreign born when it comes to educational attainment, median household income, poverty, homeownership, and residential segregation. In the case of college completion among Asians, there is little difference by nativity, as both foreign- and native-born Asians have college completion rates far above the national average (Hsin and Xie, 2014; Iceland, 2017: 79–86). Among Hispanics, while the native-born have higher levels of education and income than those born abroad, they still lag behind whites. Whether intergenerational progress will eventually lead to parity between Hispanics and whites is the subject of continued debate (Iceland, 2017; Perlmann, 2005; Telles and Ortiz, 2008).

There is a glass-half-empty/glass-half-full quality to the Social Justice and Social Order interpretations of these data on assimilation. Those from the Social Justice perspective tend to emphasize continued inequalities, and remain concerned that racism constrains upward mobility, especially among people of Hispanic origin.

They therefore seek affirmative action for under-represented groups in many organizations as a way to reduce these constraints. Meanwhile, those from the Social Order perspective are more likely to emphasize the upward mobility that many immigrant groups have achieved, and argue that this indicates that individuals from other groups may similarly seize opportunities for advancement.

## Individual and Group-Based Morality

As we have seen, advocates of the Social Justice perspective are often particularly attuned to the plight of the vulnerable and the rights of the oppressed. Their focus on *individual welfare* leads them to interpret social problems as the result of unequal or unfair treatment. Meanwhile, those from the Social Order perspective, while concerned about individual well-being, are also attuned to *societal stability and cohesion,* and thus believe that people should also behave in ways that strengthen society as a whole.

The application of the Social Justice perspective to racial inequality is straightforward: since people from under-represented groups have been marginalized by structural racism, behaving morally means taking up their plight and fighting for their well-being in a system that in many ways is rigged against them. This view is reflected in the American Civil Liberties Union briefs written in 1976 in support of affirmative action in *Regents of the University of California v. Bakke*:

> the major civil liberties issue still facing the United States is the elimination, root and branch, of all vestiges of racism. No other asserted claim of right surpasses the wholly justified demand of the nation's discrete and

insular minorities for access to the American mainstream from which they have so long been excluded (*Regents of the University of California v. Bakke*, 1978).

In contrast, the Social Order perspective seeks to balance individual well-being against society's need for order and cohesion. This perspective is therefore concerned about possible unintended consequences that may result from well-meaning interventions designed to reduce racial inequality. Some advocates have argued that affirmative action, while well-intentioned, is divisive because it generates resentment among groups that are not among the protected classes (Caldwell, 2020). Such resentment undermines social cohesion. As social commentator Coleman Hughes has argued in an analysis of the current anti-racist movement, which he refers to as a "race-conscious" vision:

> In the race-conscious vision, racial harmony is an afterthought. At times, it is actively shunned. Race-consciousness seeks to "problematize" relations between members of different ethnic groups in a variety of ways. In 2017, for instance, the *New York Times* ran an op-ed entitled "Can My Children Be Friends with White People?" written by a black father who planned on teaching his sons "to have profound doubts that friendship with white people is possible" – a near-perfect reversal of Dr. King's message. (Hughes, 2020)

The introduction of race-conscious anti-racism programming into K-12 schools likewise has generated considerable debate. These efforts have included implementing training on implicit bias, microaggressions, and culturally responsive teaching, and as such they center on a moral orientation that prioritizes the welfare of the individual. Such social-justice-based materials are being integrated more generally in the curriculum in many school districts. One example is Teaching Tolerance, a program designed by the Southern Poverty Law Center for K-12 use. Its core goals are to "foster inclusiveness, reduce bias, and promote educational equity" for students in the United States (Schleeter, 2013). The approach provides programming (i.e., "standards") in four domains – identity, diversity, justice, and action (IDJA). More specifically:

> Teaching about IDJA allows educators to engage a range of anti-bias, multicultural and social justice issues. This continuum of engagement is unique among social justice teaching materials, which tend to focus on one of two areas: either reducing prejudice or advocating collective action. Prejudice reduction seeks to minimize conflict and generally focuses on changing the attitudes and behaviors of a dominant group. Collective action challenges inequality directly by raising consciousness and focusing on improving conditions for under-represented groups. The standards recognize that, in today's diverse classrooms, students need knowledge and skills related to both prejudice reduction and collective action. (Teaching Tolerance, 2016)

Those from the Social Order perspective again point out that many of these efforts are ultimately divisive and therefore reduce social cohesion in society as a whole. For instance, in her research on some of these academic practices in action, politics of education scholar Samantha Hedges spoke to one teacher who described how she had adopted the curricular approach of elevating non-Western cultural values over Western ones. As Dr Hedges describes it, this did not go over well for many students:

> The teacher I spoke with had encountered this approach in her professional development session and described

the categories associated with Western and non-Western culture as "cultural essentialism" and "cultural flattening". She noted that the elevation of so-called non-Western over Western cultural values was creating a divide in her classroom: "Many of my white students felt that they were being blamed for society's problems just by virtue of being who they are – white, middle-class men – and frankly this kind of training would only serve to reinforce this view. This training gives no sense that Western or American culture has ever had anything valuable to contribute to the world and is nothing at all to be proud of." (Hedges, 2020)

Echoing these concerns, in December 2020, a black mother and her biracial son filed a lawsuit accusing a Las Vegas charter school of creating a hostile learning environment by requiring him to participate in the school's social justice curriculum. Their suit alleged that class assignments required students to reveal their race, gender, sexual orientation, and disabilities and then determine if privilege or oppression is attached to those identities. They also included breakout discussions that the plaintiffs said students could opt out of but which still created a "psychologically abusive dilemma" and a "hostile educational environment" (Girnus, 2021).

Those from the Social Justice perspective contend that, while there might be occasional excesses, the concerns described above are largely overblown, and students must be made to confront our history of racial inequality if we are to overcome current inequality. In a critique of bills under consideration in a few states to restrict or ban the use of critical race theory in public schools, University of Texas at Austin Deans Esther Clazada and Cossy Hough argued that "Fear is a powerful motivator. At issue seems to be the fear that white people are and will be victims in the dredging up of an unjust past.

This rhetoric of fear was on prominent display when Idaho legislators described critical race theory as 'indoctrination,' 'poison' and 'garbage'" (Calzada and Hough, 2021). Because those with a Social Justice perspective tend to rank helping the vulnerable above maintaining social cohesion in their moral framework, they tend to view such fear as a tolerable price to pay for a desirable outcome rather than as an indication that the proposed policy is producing a negative result.

## Social Change

Individuals from the Social Justice perspective tend to believe that morally enlightened policymakers are capable of fashioning a more just and equitable society without producing unintended negative consequences. Such enlightened policymakers are presumed to favor policy initiatives that do away with what they see as outmoded, and immoral, ways of structuring society and allocating resources. Regarding racial and ethnic disparities, those with a Social Justice perspective are generally dissatisfied with the traditional "colorblind" approach to promoting equality, which largely stops with the equal treatment of people under the law. Affirmative action in universities represented a significant departure from that approach by giving individuals from under-represented groups an advantage in admissions decisions.

At the heart of history professor Ibram X. Kendi's recommended approach to anti-racism (introduced in Chapter 1) is the overt use of discrimination to achieve equality of representation across racial groups in organizations. According to Kendi, "If discrimination is creating equity then it is anti-racist" (2019a: 21). More generally, proactively eradicating systemic racism is a key feature of many current Social-Justice-inspired efforts to reduce racial inequality. For instance, the University of Southern California School of Social Work includes the following description of anti-racism:

> Anti-racism is the practice of opposing and dismantling social, cultural and structural instances of racism. Being anti-racist means committing to identifying how racism manifests in social and cultural norms and how to address racism at the individual and structural levels. "The work is ongoing," said Renee Smith-Maddox, clinical professor and diversity liaison at the USC Suzanne Dworak-Peck School of Social Work. "You have to learn and unlearn some of the things that you understand about a racialized society and your role in it." No one is born a racist or anti-racist. It is a result of the history of race and racism in the United States, our experiences and the choices people make. Even when a person's biases are unconscious, their behaviors and attitudes can still be racist and wield harm against people in marginalized communities. (University of Southern California, 2020)

Those who believe in the Social Order perspective, in contrast, are more likely to believe that human nature, with its good and bad impulses, cannot fundamentally change. It follows that policy interventions that go against this, including those derived from an anti-racism orientation, are bound to fail. They also believe that the traditional liberal values on which Western democracies are based (i.e., freedom, equality, and responsibility) provide a proven framework for guiding behavior in ways that are both personally and socially beneficial. They are thus wary of efforts to rapidly change existing social practices, especially if they require deviating from these core values. In addition to the unintended consequences that rapid social change seems likely to produce, those from the Social Order perspective are also concerned about entrusting political elites with the far-reaching power to enact their social-change agenda quickly. As Coleman Hughes, in the article cited earlier, argues:

> Today, many feel that this principle [the "colorblind" approach to racial inequality] represents the very status quo that we must depart from in order to begin making progress. The goal of getting past race, in this view, is precisely what has prevented us from implementing the race-conscious policies that would meaningfully address racial inequality. But this underplays how much progress we have already made. Back in the early 1970s, the NYPD killed 91 people in a single year. In 2018, they killed five. Since 2001, the national incarceration rate for black men ages 18–29 has been cut by more than half. Most people don't know this . . . The current system, warts and all, has enabled huge progress for black people in recent decades. Overturning the liberal principles on which our institutions are based would not hasten progress towards racial equality; it would threaten the very stability that is required for incremental progress to occur. (Hughes, 2020)

Affirmative action has been at the center of debates about what to do about racial inequality for decades, as have more recent Diversity, Equity, and Inclusion (DEI) efforts. Affirmative action was first implemented as part of President John F. Kennedy's Executive Order 10925, which stated that government contractors should "take affirmative action to ensure that applicants are employed . . . without regard to their race, creed, color, or national origin" (MacLaury, 2010). Notably, this decree explicitly affirmed the traditional goal of nondiscrimination. The Civil Rights Act of 1964 took the same tack, as Title VII under this act prohibits an employer from discriminating based on the characteristics described above and prohibits preferential treatment of any group.

Despite the initial language, the following year President Lyndon Johnson pivoted toward favoring preferential treatment to equalize outcomes. Because of the disadvantages blacks faced due to the history of discrimination, Johnson asserted that special help was needed to achieve "equality as a result" and "not just legal equity" (Mills, 1994: 7).

Over the years, the US Supreme Court has ruled that some affirmative action practices are unconstitutional, including strict racial or gender quotas for college admissions and jobs. In addition, employers generally are not allowed to hire individual candidates on the basis of their race or gender, except in rare cases and only as a temporary measure to address severe past job segregation or discrimination (Reskin, 1998: 15–17). With regards to higher education, a series of Supreme Court decisions ruled that race can play at least some role in the admissions policies of public universities. For example, in *Grutter v. Bollinger* (2003), the Court ruled that race could be taken into account in holistic evaluations of individual student applicants that also took into account other factors such as grades and extracurricular activities.

Many public and private organizations today actively seek to increase diversity in a variety of ways. For instance, most prominent universities have a large and growing number of administrators devoted to issues of DEI. Many DEI initiatives are modeled on pre-existing affirmative action programs, as one of their main missions is to increase the diversity of the faculty and students (Mac Donald, 2018).

Some DEI initiatives take existing affirmative action programs in new directions. The "E" in DEI – "Equity" – emphasizes equality not just of opportunity, which was the defining feature of the Civil Rights Act, but also equality of outcomes, as favored by President Johnson and other supporters of affirmative action over the years. Many universities now require faculty applicants to submit DEI statements. The University of California San Diego, for example, states that "All candidates applying for faculty appointments at UC San Diego are required to submit a personal statement on their contributions to diversity, regardless of personal characteristics. The purpose of the statement is to identify candidates who have the professional skills, experience, and/or willingness to engage in activities that will advance institutional diversity and equity goals" (UC San Diego, 2021).

Programs to increase diversity extend to the private sector as well. The tech industry has long been criticized as being too white (and Asian) and male. Thus, most large tech companies have affirmative action policies in place to recruit women and people from under-represented groups. Google, for example, issues an annual diversity report to keep track of recruiting efforts and requires that employees take unconscious bias training, with the thinking that unconscious bias is one of the main factors that limits diversity.

Some have argued that Google has been too zealous in its efforts, and the company was the target of a 2018 lawsuit alleging discrimination in hiring. The lawsuit included allegations that recruiting teams were instructed by a hiring manager to reject white and Asian male candidates. The dispute was ultimately sent to arbitration (Mulvaney, 2020).

With a similar goal of equity, in 2021 Congress passed and President Biden signed a COVID relief bill that gave priority status for COVID-19 relief to restaurants and bars owned by women and certain minority groups. However, a US Appeals Court ruled, in *Vitolo et al. v. Guzman*, that this law, by discriminating on the basis of race, was unconstitutional (Reynolds, 2021). New DEI initiatives face the tension of increasing diversity while not discriminating against people who are not members of protected groups. This tension has meant that new initiatives have resulted in a number of recent lawsuits alleging reverse discrimination (Mulvaney, 2020). It is likely that debates about these kinds of programs will continue, especially on the grounds of fairness as described above.

Differing views about the possibility of successfully engineering social change also influence the debate about traditional affirmative action programs. Regarding their effectiveness in diversifying organizations, research has shown that they have moderately increased the representation of minority groups and women in universities and private sector employment (Holzer and Neumark, 2000, 2006; Urofsky, 2020: 147–148 and 209–210). The programs' effects have perhaps been greatest in academia, where there has been a marked increase in the representation of blacks and Hispanics in elite universities and graduate courses (Bowen et al., 1999; Hinrichs, 2012; Holzer and Neumark, 2006). Immigrants and their children have also benefited considerably from affirmative action. Currently, immigrants and their children are over-represented among minority group members that are admitted to elite universities (Kasinitz et al., 2008; Massey et al., 2003; Mooney et al., 2007). Those with a Social Justice perspective are likely to view these procedures favorably because of how they evaluate fairness – as the degree to which outcomes are proportionally distributed across racial groups.

In contrast, those with a Social Order perspective tend to argue that, despite the changes described above, affirmative action may often unintentionally harm its intended beneficiaries. One concern along these lines is that affirmative action may produce a "mismatch" between the preparation and skill of those who benefit from the policy and the preparation and skill expected in the contexts in which the beneficiaries find themselves. When it comes to college admissions, for instance, the difference in standardized test scores at admission between applicants who are likely to benefit from affirmative action and those who are not can be substantial. The average SAT score (math + verbal) for African Americans and Hispanics entering Duke University in 2001 and 2002 was, respectively, 140 points and 70 points lower than the average for white students (Arcidiacono et al., 2011).

These differences raise important questions. How should we evaluate the costs and benefits of placing students and employees into competitive roles for which they may be ill-prepared compared to their colleagues? How should we think about the costs and benefits of policies that advantage some groups and disadvantage others?

Evidence that mismatch causes important negative outcomes is mixed. As evidence against this theory, Espenshade and Radford (2009) found that minority students who benefited from affirmative action were *more* likely to graduate when attending elite institutions than when they attended other universities. They attribute this in part to the fact that elite universities have more resources for students and higher graduation rates overall than other kinds of universities. Evidence supporting the theory suggests that minority students admitted because of affirmative action are *more* likely to graduate lower in their class. Student beneficiaries of affirmative action also tend to switch from more demanding majors, such as those in STEM, to less demanding majors prior to graduation (Arcidiacono et al., 2016). Switching to less demanding majors could contribute to the under-representation of minority groups in prestigious and highly remunerated occupations.

While those from the Social Justice perspective tend to favor affirmative action policies and initiatives to increase diversity (i.e., DEI initiatives), those from the Social Order perspective tend to object to DEI initiatives that are informed by critical race theory. They see them as undermining the liberal values that are central to the founding principles of the country, most notably the principle of equal treatment by the law. Many with a Social Order perspective fear that undermining such principles threatens the order and cohesion of society. They are also concerned that the cultural ascendance of DEI thinking is having a cooling effect on expressions of dissent. As former philosophy professor Peter Boghossian argues:

> Social Justice is a dangerous, illiberal ideology that is taking over society. Although often associated with "liberalism" in the United States, it is explicitly anti-liberal. One of the core pillars of Critical Race Theory, upon which one dimension of Social Justice ideology rests, is a critique of liberalism, where "critique" is meant as Karl Marx used it and "liberalism" is the broad philosophy of individual liberty upon which the United States was founded. One of the easiest ways to understand how illiberal Social Justice can be is available to anyone who attempts to criticize it. Those who criticize Social Justice are not thanked for helping to improve its tenets. Rather, they're called bigots, homophobes, Nazis, grifters, misogynists, or, the trump card meant to silence all conversation: racists ... As Social Justice creeps into everything and rewrites it with illiberalism, accusations, unfairness, and a conspicuous refusal to have a reasoned conversation about anything it proposes, we put ourselves and our societies at tremendous risk of losing

the norms civil society needs to function. (Boghossian, 2020)

Those from the Social Justice perspective, however, believe new approaches to increasing DEI are essential for change, even in the face of considerable opposition. As Tonia Wellons, writing for the sociology journal *Contexts*, argues:

> As a racial equity tool, affirmative action is a full-circle opportunity. Even as we try our best to win hearts and minds with equality arguments, research continues to demonstrate the persistence of racism and the vestiges of a dark, but not so distant history of mass exploitation and abuse. Today, I take a lot of pride in my seat at the table, in being regarded as an equal with people whose early beginnings looked so different from my own. That is what affirmative action was designed to achieve, and I will continue to uphold it as a tool for racial equity until full equality is achieved. (Wellons, 2019: 80)

## *Conclusion*

Even if there were no competing perspectives to navigate, adjudicating between the proposed causes of racial inequality in the United States and the consequences of affirmative action interventions designed to ameliorate it would be no easy task. Systemic racism – inequality's primary cause according to those with the Social Justice perspective – is notoriously difficult to observe and measure. This makes it nearly impossible to distinguish from other possible causes. Culture practices and individual agency – the primary causes according to those from the Social Order perspective – are also difficult to measure and therefore distinguish from other possible causes. The consequences of affirmative action interventions, which can range from achieving proportional representation to ensuring that preferred groups thrive in the educational and work settings into which they are selected, are also difficult to parse out.

As a result, even when social scientists devise studies that measure as well as they can the various possible contributing factors and relevant consequences, their conclusions are fraught. The methods can always be criticized by the opposing side for failing to account for factors that would have produced results more favorable to their position. We are thus again left in a sort of limbo from which data alone cannot, as of yet, free us. Liberation from this limbo will only be achieved when we set our sights on recognizing and taking seriously the different assumptions intrinsic to these two perspectives. In the next chapter, we examine the role of the Social Justice and Social Order perspectives in shaping current debates about income inequality and poverty in the US.

# 5

# Income Inequality and Poverty

---

Income inequality has risen since 1980, making it a topic of great interest and concern among academics, the media, and the public (McCall and Percheski, 2010). The Occupy Wall Street movement in 2011, which emerged in the aftermath of the preceding years' recession, was a highly visible manifestation of this concern. The continued struggle of many working families to make ends meet, along with increased homelessness in large US cities such as San Francisco and Los Angeles, have also raised concerns (Batko et al., 2020).

While people from all perspectives would like to see everyone better off, poverty and high levels of income inequality are particularly intolerable to people with a Social Justice orientation. They see income inequality as the result of an unfair economic system that needs to be corrected. They see inequality reducing the range of choices and opportunities for the poor and members of the working class, and harming individuals in a variety of ways, including by undermining their physical and mental health. For these reasons, proponents of Social Justice argue that bold redistributive measures are required to reduce inequality and poverty. As data scientist and public commentator Sean McElwee argued in *Salon*:

Consider also this: The rise of income inequality and wealth inequality are intimately connected, and cause all sorts of problems over the long term ... The rich make enough money to save; in contrast middle-class and low-income workers don't have enough money to live, so they are increasingly burdened by debt. They can't build up wealth, which means they are deprived of opportunity. This creates a self-perpetuating cycle of wealth on the top and debt on the bottom. (McElwee, 2014)

In contrast, those from the Social Order perspective see some degree of inequality as a natural and inevitable part of any economic system. They believe that, in a market economy, inequality is not only inevitable, but also fair, because it reflects the fact that those who work hard can be rewarded for their achievements. Inequality is therefore to be expected whenever individuals are granted the freedom to pursue their goals. In a market system, economic incentives that produce inequality are seen as good for society because those same incentives spur innovation and the creation of valued goods and services, ranging from powerful computing devices to new medicines that save lives. From this perspective, redistributive policies, while well meaning, are to be used judiciously because they disincentivize hard work and innovation. English Professor Neema Parvini articulated many elements of this view in *Quillette*:

Is it fair that [singer and songwriter] Adele's net worth is $135 million while mine is at least 270 times less than that? How many people want to watch Adele in concert and how many want to see me in concert? Her net productivity because of this demand, and her net contribution to the economy, is therefore many times greater than mine – and so it is entirely fair that she should earn that much more. This is not to mention how many hundreds of people – managers, marketing executives, roadies, theatre managers and so on – are employed because of the demand for Adele's singing talents, whereas the total number of people directly employed because of me is considerably less. (Parvini, 2018)

In this chapter, we discuss how the Social Order and Social Justice framework is useful for understanding divergent views about poverty and inequality in the United States today. As in previous chapters, we organize our discussion around differences between those who favor a Social Justice versus a Social Order perspective with respect to: fairness and equality; freedom, choice, and responsibility; individual and group-based morality; and attitudes toward social change.

As described in early chapters, it is important to note that our book describes the contours of the Social Order and Social Justice perspectives in the contemporary United States. With regards to economic matters, proponents of Social Order in the US typically favor economic liberalism (or "neoliberalism," according to critics), as championed by President Ronald Reagan and most conservative politicians and commentators since. In other countries, proponents of Social Order on cultural issues and immigration sometimes advocate for economically redistributive policies. It is conceivable that we may see this approach more frequently in the future among Social Order proponents in the United States.

## Fairness and Equality

Fairness, according to the Social Justice perspective, is primarily determined by whether there are relatively equal outcomes across groups. While most reasonable

111

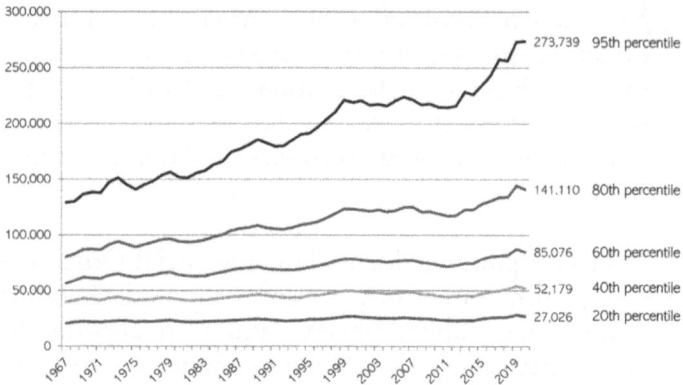

**Figure 5.1** Household incomes by quintile, 1967–2020
(2020 dollars)

*Source:* Data from US Census Bureau, 2020c

people recognize that equality across every individual, family, community, or nation is neither possible nor desirable, those from the Social Justice perspective are alarmed by high, and increasing, levels of income inequality and the poverty that often accompanies it. Let's look at the data on inequality and poverty that raise this concern.

While economic growth in the US over the past several decades has increased household incomes and standards of living, income inequality also has risen. Figure 5.1 provides a visual representation of this trend by showing the distribution of household income over the 1967 to 2020 period (in 2020 dollars). While the income of all groups rose over the period, the increase was largest for the highest-income households. For example, the income for households at the 95th percentile more than doubled, from $129,105 in 1967 to $273,739 in 2020. For those at the 80th percentile, incomes rose by 75 percent (from $80,453 to $141,110). Meanwhile, income for households at the 20th percentile rose by just 33

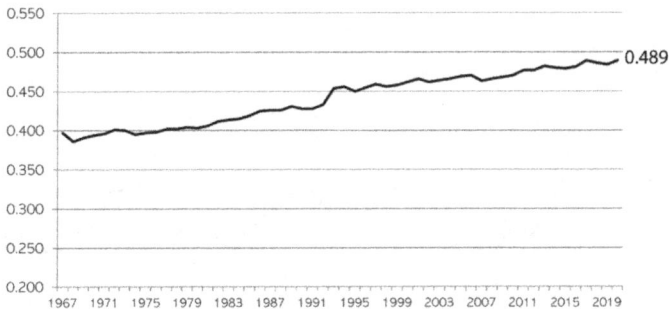

**Figure 5.2**   Gini coefficient for inequality in household
income, 1967–2020

*Source:* Data from US Census Bureau, 2020d

percent, from $20,385 to $27,026 (US Census Bureau,
2020c).

A common way of measuring inequality is to use
the Gini coefficient. The Gini coefficient can be used to
measure inequality in a community, a state, a country, or
any other level of aggregation. The Gini coefficient can
range from 0 to 1. Regarding household income, a Gini
coefficient of 0 means that all households have the same
income and 1 means that one household possesses all the
income while the rest have none. Figure 5.2 shows that
the Gini coefficient for US households increased steadily
over much of the 1967 to 2020 period, from 0.397 in
1967 to 0.489 in 2020 (US Census Bureau, 2020d).

Inequality in wealth is even more dramatic. Wealth
includes a wide array of assets in addition to income,
such as homes, savings accounts, retirement accounts,
and stocks and bonds. Many Americans have no wealth
or savings at all, while others are extraordinarily
wealthy. The share of aggregate wealth held by upper-
income families increased from 60 percent in 1983 to 79
percent in 2016 (Horowitz et al., 2020).

113

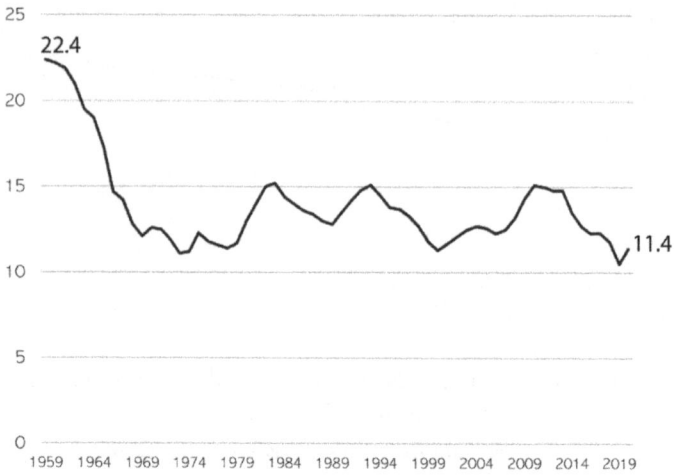

**Figure 5.3**   Official poverty rate, 1959–2020
*Source:* Data from US Census Bureau, 2020a

According to the official US poverty measure, which gauges the proportion of people with incomes below an inflation-adjusted threshold in a given year ($26,172 for a family of four in 2019), poverty declined considerably from 1959 (the first year of the official time series) until the early 1970s (see Figure 5.3). Since then, it has fluctuated with the economic cycle – increasing during recessions and declining during periods of growth. In 2019, after a decade of near continuous economic growth (and before the COVID-19 pandemic), the poverty rate, at 10.5 percent, was at a historic low (Iceland, 2013; Semega et al., 2020). The poverty rate increased to 11.4 in the 2020 pandemic year (Shrider et al., 2021). This means that poverty had declined somewhat even as income inequality increased. In this case, the increase in income inequality was mainly a function of the rich gaining income at a faster rate than did the poor.

It is important to note that some of the patterns and trends in poverty and inequality we've described here are themselves in dispute. Some researchers argue that statistics on income inequality gathered from household surveys (such as those shown in the figures above) overstate its increase over time because the measure of income used does not take into account taxes people pay or some of the various government transfers, such as Medicare, Medicaid, and Supplementary Nutrition Assistance, that people receive (Gramm and Early, 2021). These omissions are potentially problematic because higher-income people tend to pay more in taxes and receive fewer transfers while lower-income people tend to pay less in taxes and receive more transfers. Unsurprisingly, adjusting for tax payments and transfers reduces estimates of income inequality, and studies that make these adjustments tend to find smaller increases in income inequality over time than those done using government statistics that do not make these adjustments (Auten and Splinter, 2019; Larrimore et al., 2021; Saez and Zucman, 2020).

Analysts also debate about how best to measure trends in poverty. People tend to under-report income in surveys, and tax returns are a weak source of data since many low-income people do not submit them. While scholars relying on government data that do not take these factors into account argue that extreme poverty has increased, others using detailed administrative data conclude that extreme poverty has declined (Edin and Shaefer, 2015; Meyer et al., 2021).

These discrepancies matter for how we think about inequality generally. People with a Social Justice perspective often highlight statistics that show high levels of poverty and inequality, perhaps to elicit more concern about the issue from the public. Meanwhile, those with a Social Order perspective are more likely to highlight statistics that downplay inequality as a problem, possibly because of their concerns about the enactment of redistributive policies that would reduce incentives to work.

Returning to the issue of fairness, many of those from the Social Justice perspective, who see poverty and inequality as fundamentally unfair, tend to state their arguments for redistributive change in moral terms, often equating inequality with oppression. As sociologist Matthew Desmond argues:

> We need a new language for talking about poverty. "Nobody who works should be poor," we say. That's not good enough. Nobody in America should be poor, period. No single mother struggling to raise children on her own; no formerly incarcerated man who has served his time; no young heroin user struggling with addiction and pain; no retired bus driver whose pension was squandered; nobody. And if we respect hard work, then we should reward it, instead of deploying this value to shame the poor and justify our unconscionable and growing inequality. (Desmond, 2018)

Others from the Social Justice perspective take a somewhat different approach. They argue that our economic system itself is unfair, not so much because of poverty or inequality per se, but because the rich wield disproportionate power. They argue that our economic system allows the rich to make rules that enhance their wealth and influence. The rich are also described as increasing their wealth at the expense of those in the middle and the bottom, such as by holding down the wages of their workers to reap greater profit. As public policy professor and former Secretary of Labor Robert Reich writes:

> Those with great wealth have translated it into political power. And with that power they've busted labor unions (to which a third of private-sector workers belonged in the 1950s but now fewer than 7 percent do), halved the

taxes they pay (from a top marginal rate of 91 percent in the 1950s to 39 percent today, and from an effective rate of 52 percent then to 18 percent now), cut safety nets, deregulated Wall Street, privatized much of the economy, expanded bankruptcy protection for themselves while narrowing it for you, forced you into mandatory arbitration of employment disputes, expanded their patents and intellectual property, got trade deals that benefited them but squeezed your pay and concentrated their market power so you pay more for pharmaceuticals, health insurance, airfare, food, internet service and much else. (Reich, 2016)

As we have shown, however, many from the Social Order perspective do not see inequality as being in itself evidence of unfairness. Instead, inequality is expected in a system that rewards people for the value that they produce. In this view, a fair system is one whose rules apply evenly to everyone. As economics professor Steven Horwitz has argued:

If people really care about fairness, then supporters of the market should be insisting on the importance of equality before the law. If we really did want to create a world of equal outcomes, we would have to penalize the productive in various ways, and we would have to provide unequal benefits to those who were less productive. In the extreme, we end up in the world of Kurt Vonnegut's Harrison Bergeron, where the state constructs individualized forms of interference to hamper the skilled, such as buzzers in the ears of the intelligent or weights on the limbs of the strong. Equality of outcomes requires that we treat people differently, and this will likely be perceived as unfair by many. Equality before the law corresponds better with notions of fairness even if the outcomes it produces are unequal. (Horwitz, 2017)

Moreover, those from the Social Order perspective often distinguish between inequality generated by innovation, which is seen as fair and even beneficial for society, versus inequality that comes from corruption or from the reduction of competition that otherwise would lower prices and incentivize the production of value. Economist David R. Henderson of the Hoover Institution provides the following examples to highlight this distinction:

> Consider another example – two of the richest people in the world are Bill Gates and Carlos Slim. Gates got rich by starting and building Microsoft, whose main product, an operating system for personal computers, made life better for the rest of us. Would you have a well-functioning personal computer if Bill Gates hadn't existed? Yes. But his existence and his clear thinking early on hastened the PC revolution by at least a year. That might not sound like a lot, but each gain we consumers got from each step of the PC revolution occurred a year earlier because of Bill Gates. Over 40 years, that amounts to trillions of dollars in value to consumers ... Mexican multi-billionaire Carlos Slim is currently the seventh-richest man in the world. He got rich the way Lyndon Johnson got rich. The Mexican government handed him a monopoly on telecommunications in Mexico and he uses it to charge high prices for phone calls. Slim is clearly exacerbating income inequality in a way that makes other people poorer. (Henderson, 2018)

Those from the Social Order and Social Justice perspectives generally agree that a system that offers different rules for different people is unfair. However, they differ in whether income inequality by itself should be viewed as an indication that the system that produced it is unfair.

## *Freedom, Choice, and Responsibility*

A person with a Social Justice perspective often measures freedom in terms of power and influence. Inequality is thought to constrain both for low-income people, thus limiting their ability to flourish. On average, children growing up in poor families perform worse in school, show weaker cognitive development, and have poorer mental health than those growing up in non-poor families. They are also less likely to achieve financial success than those born into richer families. As adults, those who are poor are more likely to have health problems and die at younger ages (Iceland, 2013).

For these reasons, economist and Nobel Prize winner Amartya Sen argues that poverty itself should be conceived as "capability deprivation," because it prevents people from living the kind of life that would bring them happiness. Writing in 1999, he noted that "capability deprivation" is more likely to occur when there are high levels of inequality:

> [R]elative deprivation in terms of *incomes* can yield *absolute* deprivation in terms of *capabilities*. Being relatively poor in a rich country can be a great capability handicap, even when one's absolute income is high in terms of world standards. In a generally opulent country, more income is needed to buy enough commodities to achieve *the same social functioning* . . . The need to take part in the life of a community may induce demands for modern equipment (televisions, videocassette recorders, automobiles and so on) in a country where such facilities are more or less universal (unlike what would be needed in less affluent countries), and this imposes a strain on a relatively poor person in a rich country even when that person is at a much higher level of income compared

119

> with people in less opulent counties. (Sen, 1999: 89–90;
> emphases in the original).

Inequality is thus a form of oppression. Moreover, it reduces the range of choices and capabilities people have in the types of work they must accept to survive, and it reduces the goods they can purchase based on that work. Because the poor must routinely submit to the will of others, they develop lower levels of self-efficacy, which exacerbates the problem. As economics and humanistic studies professor Marc Fleurbaey argues, "Since in all poverty (or even inequality) there is oppression, the fundamental right to personal integrity can only be respected by introducing a right to escape poverty" (Fleurbaey, 2007: 154).

According to this view, it is pragmatic to redistribute wealth from the rich, as the loss of income from higher taxation will make little difference to the lives of those at the top but would significantly improve the well-being of those in the middle and bottom of the income distribution (Oxfam, 2022).

In contrast, many who hold the Social Order perspective believe that freedom implies the ability to succeed, or fail, based on one's abilities and effort. For instance, in a rebuttal to Desmond's opinion piece on poverty cited above, columnist Mona Charen, writing for *National Review*, argues that, in discussing the struggles of a poor woman named Vanessa at one point in his story, Desmond underplays how poor choices can exacerbate poverty. She writes:

> It may well be true that low-level, unskilled jobs are less of a ladder out of poverty than they once were. But the other aspect of Vanessa's plight, and that of her children, Desmond and most analysts resolutely refuse to grapple with. It's familial. We learn that the father of two of her children has made erratic child-support

payments, and apart from one trip to Chuck E. Cheese, has played no role in his children's lives. The father of the youngest was sent to prison when she was 1, released when she was 8, and murdered shortly thereafter. There is no indication that Vanessa was ever married. Work is available in America, but for those with low skills and major family responsibilities, one income is simply not enough, especially for three children. According to US News and World Report, home health aides average $23,600 per year. If two home health aides are married, they earn enough to be comfortably in the middle class. (Charen, 2018)

Those who have the Social Order perspective generally acknowledge that luck, including bad luck, plays a role in how people fare in life. People lucky enough to be born into an affluent family undoubtedly have advantages over those not so lucky. However, most proponents of Social Order would argue that, insofar as social mobility is possible, people, including poor people, need to be held accountable for the choices they make, including what they do with whatever amount of "luck" has been afforded them. They might point out that most children from poor families do not grow up to be poor, even though their overall chances of becoming poor as adults are higher than for those from non-poor families (Wagmiller Jr. and Adelman, 2009).

Experts, however, disagree about the likelihood that children in the US will fare better economically than their parents. Much of this disagreement comes from the technical issues involved in measuring of the concept of "intergenerational mobility." According to one common estimate, in recent years, about 42 percent of children from families in the very low (5th) income percentile will stay in the bottom 20 percent of the income distribution as adults, while about 24 percent will rise

121

to the top half of the income distribution (Solon, 2017). This indicates a moderate amount of *relative* income mobility for those with low incomes, and more modest than in many other rich countries (Corak et al., 2014; Torche, 2015). Relative income mobility refers to the extent to which people move up or down from their starting place in the income distribution.

Measures of *absolute* mobility tell a moderately different story. Absolute mobility refers to whether children have higher income than their parents. Because standards of living have generally increased over time, absolute upward mobility across generations has been the norm. While it may have slowed in recent decades due to more modest economic growth, absolute upward mobility is still more common than absolute downward mobility across generations (Berman, 2018; Fisher and Johnson, 2020; Justman and Stiassnie, 2021).

Some scholars of poverty will point out that the historical context matters. Because of overall increases in standards of living and support from government and nonprofit organizations, what it means to be poor today is very different compared to the standards of 150 years ago. At that time, it was not uncommon for poor people in large cities to be living in crowded tenements without indoor plumbing. Likewise, poverty in the United States is qualitatively different from poverty in poor, developing countries today, where many poor people struggle mightily to meet their basic needs (Iceland, 2013).

Others are quick to say that historical comparisons set the bar too low, and having indoor plumbing should no longer be considered a sufficient indicator of being out of dire poverty. This is to say that, when standards of living increase, they should increase across the board. The boundaries and limits of this claim are clearly open for debate. Regardless of these debates, however, the strongest evidence suggests that after accounting for the under-reporting of income, extreme poverty in the United States is rare by both historical and international standards (Meyer et al., 2021).

Those from the Social Order perspective are likely to view low levels of extreme poverty and significant levels of absolute upward mobility as evidence that people who work hard and make good choices have opportunities to succeed. They see those who become poor for one reason or another as having access to sufficient resources to avoid the worst deprivations. As economist Thomas Sowell argues, "If poverty meant what most people think of as poverty – people 'ill-clad, ill-housed, and ill-nourished,' in Franklin D. Roosevelt's phrase – there would not be nearly enough people in poverty today to justify the vastly expanded powers and runaway spending of the federal government" (Sowell, 2011). For those from a Social Justice perspective, however, the fact that there is still any poverty at all, or that some people are born into better economic circumstances than others, are themselves causes for concern.

## *Individual and Group-Based Morality*

The Social Justice perspective emphasizes individual-based morality, meaning that it focuses on the prevention of individual harm, especially to those considered vulnerable. With regards to income inequality and poverty, those from the Social Justice perspective focus on the plight of the poor and their struggles to make ends meet. They argue that we need to do more to address the structural factors that lead to poverty and provide more help to individuals to alleviate their suffering. This view was stated clearly in the passage from Matthew Desmond quoted earlier in this chapter, and it is the dominant view in the writings of Social Justice proponents. The following excerpt from an article describing the plight of a woman in poverty documents this further:

> Wanda Cobb faced a . . . dilemma as the single mother of three children under 12. The best-paying job she could find, at $12 an hour, was working security at a casino. But she was on the late shift and that meant a third of her earnings went to pay for after school childcare, and even more on school breaks. Eventually, she was able to move to the day shift. "That saved a ton of money right there, and I get to see the children more. I can be there for them when they get home from school," said Cobb, who is raising her children on her own after leaving an abusive relationship. But it's a constant struggle to provide and pay the bills. "There's a lot of stress. At night you should be resting and you're laying up there thinking about how you're going to pay the bills, and it's hard to fall asleep. I started having seizures," she said. (McGreal, 2019)

While government programs help many low-income families, those from the Social Justice perspective believe that the safety net remains inadequate, as this news story recounts:

> Georgia Christensen of Sioux Falls wants to welcome her new baby into a stable environment and couldn't do that without aid from SNAP [Supplemental Nutrition Assistance Program] and other government programs. Christensen has a learning disability that makes it tough to hold a job; she said she lost her $11-an-hour position cleaning offices last year because her boss said she moved too slowly. Her husband is also out of work. Together, they are raising a teenage girl and have a baby due this month. Christensen said she isn't sure how the family would get by without her $252 monthly food stamp allotment and the $741 monthly disability payment she

receives from Social Security. "We run out towards the end of the month. It's a struggle, and I do worry," said Christensen, 34, who also visits local food pantries if necessary. (Pfankuch, 2019)

The Social Justice perspective sees these stories as evidence that the system isn't doing enough to support and assist the poor. The Social Order perspective, on the other hand, holds that while assistance to support struggling individuals is important, it must be weighed against what's best for society, as well as for individuals themselves over the long run. With regards to poverty and income inequality, the main concern among Social Order proponents is that large welfare states that provide assistance that is not tied to responsibilities create disincentives to work. They see these policies as having long-term negative impacts on the individual's work ethic, as well as on the broader economic vitality and functioning of society. Economists Leszek Balcerowicz and Marke Radzikowski summarize this concern as follows:

> There are many criticisms of the welfare state ... The economic criticism of the welfare state ultimately focuses on its negative impact on the long-run economic growth. The intermediate variables are the tax burden, reduced private savings, reduced employment, and chronic fiscal fragility or outright fiscal crises. The moral criticism shows how the repeated deviant behavior (using or misusing various social benefits) erodes social norms such as honesty, a strong work ethic, and family values. (Balcerowicz and Radzikowski, 2018)

Economist and philosophy professor James Otteson similarly critiques the welfare state, relying on arguments that highlight concerns with the degradation of the social order:

The welfare state encourages people to ignore, to violate – even to pretend does not exist – the moral principle that it is wrong to live at other people's expense. That is a fundamental pillar of an enlightened moral life – indeed what distinguishes a barbaric social order from a civilized one . . . But the welfare state seems to have clouded this central moral principle. Indeed, it seems it has entirely inverted it, even institutionalized its perversion. It has created a legal apparatus that allows, even encourages, some to live at others' expense, and this apparatus has given rise to the feeling among increasingly many people that they have the right – that they are "entitled," perhaps as a matter of "social justice" – to live at others' expense. (Otteson, 2011)

## Social Change

Individuals from the Social Justice perspective generally believe that morally enlightened policymakers should strive to fashion a more just and equitable society. They favor redistributive policies that involve progressive taxation of individuals and business. Progressive taxation refers to taxing wealthier individuals at a higher tax rate. In this scenario, low-income individuals often pay lower income taxes (and may in fact get money back in the form of a tax credit), though they do pay other kinds of taxes, such as sales taxes and, if they work, payroll taxes. Those from the Social Justice perspective often propose investing tax dollars in institutions that provide broad support to all members of society and/or transferring those funds directly to those in need.

Those from the Social Justice perspective justify these transfers on several grounds, including that they are a necessary corrective to an unfair economic system that favors the wealthy (as described above) and that it is a moral imperative to help the less fortunate. They favor policies that strengthen the social safety net. This includes child credits for families, universal health insurance, free and universal preschool provision, and access to free college, among other programs. They often point to successful welfare states as role models, such as Scandinavian countries, where high taxes fund numerous programs that provide relief to low-income families. Indeed, cross-national comparisons show that poverty in the United States, measured as the proportion of people with incomes that are less than half the median income in a given country, is higher than in most rich peer countries in the OECD (Organisation for Economic Co-operation and Development) (OECD, 2021). As history professor Colin Gordon argues: "The American welfare state is widely regarded as a poor cousin to those of its democratic peers. As the most unequal wealthy country, the United States also does the least to address that inequality through public policy – despite strong historical and international evidence that social spending programs can drastically reduce inequality" (Gordon, 2014).

Some proponents of Social Justice favor providing a universal basic income (UBI) to all Americans as another way to address inequality and bolster the social safety net. Several countries – including the United States, Canada, Germany, Finland, India, and China – have experimented or are experimenting with such programs in targeted localities. While the design and level of support provided by UBI programs varies, one example of a proposal came from Andrew Yang. In his unsuccessful run for US president in 2020, he proposed providing $1,000 per month to every American adult. He called this a "Freedom Dividend" that would "enable all Americans to pay their bills, educate themselves, start a business, be more creative, stay healthy, relocate for work, spend time with their children, take care of loved ones, and have a real stake in the future" (Yang, 2019). Many from the Social Justice perspective believe that this kind of cash transfer, along with others such as free preschool education and college tuition, would reduce barriers to mobility and expand access to opportunity.

Conversely, many people with a Social Order orientation are wary of the degree of social engineering required to bring forth a more equitable and robust society. A prominent concern with the expansion of the welfare state is the long-term behavioral response such expansion seems likely to produce. As noted earlier, from this perspective, cash transfers disincentivize work and foster an attitude of entitlement. Such policies also undermine key social institutions that have traditionally provided support, such as strong families and cohesive communities. Indeed, Social Order-minded critics of the welfare state point to the historic increase in single-parenthood that occurred as the welfare state grew (Murray, 2012). And taxes and transfer payments from the government to individual citizens may also reduce overall well-being. Such policies take money (in the form of taxes) from more productive members of society, who could otherwise invest it in useful and innovative products and services, and give it to less productive individuals.

While many of those from the Social Order perspective would acknowledge that government transfers reduce poverty and increase economic security in the short run, they worry about the long-term economic and social costs. As researcher Robert Rector of the conservative Heritage Foundation argued:

> Historically, marriage has played a critical role in the raising of children. In most cases, the economic benefits of marriage are substantial. Marriage among families with children is an extremely powerful factor in promoting

economic self-sufficiency: the ability of families to support themselves above poverty without reliance on government means-tested welfare aid ... Marriage is good for children, mothers, and fathers, but marriage is disappearing in low-income communities. In part, this is due to the fact that the U.S. welfare system actively penalizes many low-income parents who do marry. The anti-marriage incentives built into the welfare state are indefensible. Policymakers should reduce welfare's anti-marriage penalties. (Rector, 2014)

A similar concern has been raised about UBI proposals. Professor Clay Routledge and his colleague Gonazalo Schwarz argue that giving money to people with no strings attached will create disincentives to work that ultimately reduce individual and societal well-being:

UBI seems like a simple way to make people's lives easier and to defend against fears of a future without work. However, a life without work is not a recipe for human flourishing. Humans are at their best when they are creating, building, experimenting, innovating and focusing on ways they can make a difference in the world. We should be very cautious about taking actions that could undermine such ambitions. (Routledge and Schwarz, 2021)

In short, those from the Social Justice perspective argue that swift and extensive action is needed to reduce inequality and poverty. They often see those from the Social Order perspective as reactionary or as apologists for the wealthy. In contrast, those from the Social Order perspective are wary of the long-term impact of far-reaching redistributive policies. They believe such policies cause problems in the long run in the form of reduced innovation and growth. They often see those from the Social Justice perspective as idealists who downplay both the frailties of human nature and the disincentives to productive living contained within the well-meaning policies they propose.

## Conclusion

Poverty and inequality exist to varying degrees in every known society. However, the degree to which poverty and inequality are natural outgrowths of a well-functioning, competitive economic system, or symptoms of a broken, exploitative one, has been the subject of debate for centuries. From a Social Justice perspective, the suffering implied by poverty and inequality requires immediate action if we are to maintain our status as a moral nation. From a Social Order perspective, poverty and inequality are to be expected as people sort themselves through fair competition based on their talents and efforts. Artificially altering this sorting undermines our status as a moral nation.

We are thus once again brought to an impasse from which data alone cannot release us. The only way forward is to recognize the different assumptions regarding fairness and equality; freedom, choice, and responsibility; individual and group-based morality; and attitudes toward social change that those with a Social Justice or a Social Order perspective use to interpret the available data to arrive at an understanding of the world around them. Rather than spend time fighting about whose assumptions are correct, as if reality were reducible to a single view, we need to develop and institutionalize methods for balancing the insights of both perspectives. In the final chapter of this book, we provide some ideas for achieving this balance. But first, we take a look at a final issue has garnered a great amount of attention both historically and in recent years: immigration.

# 6

# Immigration

---

Nearly 45 million immigrants lived in the United States in 2019, a historic high. The percentage of the US population that is foreign-born, at nearly 14 percent, is much higher than the nearly 5 percent that was foreign-born in 1970, though still short of the record high of the nearly 15 percent who were foreign born in 1890, when the US population as a whole was a lot smaller (Batlova et al., 2021). The United States is by far the top destination of immigrants worldwide, with over three times more immigrants than the next largest immigrant-receiving country (Germany) (Migration Policy Institute, 2021).

Immigration is a polarizing topic in the United States and people frame the debate about immigration in the US in very different ways. Those from the Social Justice perspective are more likely to favor policies that increase immigration. They are also more likely to favor assisting immigrants who have suffered economic, political, or social hardships in their home countries. They often support generous refugee policies and policies that provide a path to citizenship for unauthorized immigrants. Further, they seek to reduce barriers to mobility and social inequality that immigrants may face.

Those from the Social Justice perspective also generally see immigration, the diversity it brings, and the country's willingness to do the right thing by welcoming immigrants, as a source of national strength. As the website for the International Rescue Committee, a non-profit group dedicated to responding to humanitarian crises, asserted in 2021:

> The United States has long offered safe haven to people fleeing violence, tyranny and persecution. After four years of record-low arrivals under the Trump Administration, President Joe Biden has an opportunity to rebuild America's bipartisan tradition of welcoming refugees. This is not just a lifesaving humanitarian imperative at a time when more people worldwide are uprooted by war and crisis than ever before. Refugee resettlement also enriches our economy and enhances our national security. (International Rescue Committee, 2021)

In contrast, those from the Social Order perspective express concern with the potentially destabilizing aspects of high levels of immigration. They argue that high levels of immigration, especially unauthorized immigration, reduce job opportunities and wages for native-born workers. They also argue that immigration creates other serious challenges, including imposing fiscal costs on localities that must provide additional education and health-care services to immigrants, destabilizing communities that must struggle to integrate newcomers, and increasing crime and violence in some places. In addition, many Social Order proponents assert that unauthorized immigration by its very nature undermines the rule of law. As the Heritage Foundation, a conservative think tank, contends:

> The debate is not about whether we should allow immigration – it's about how we do so in a way that protects American sovereignty, respects the rule of law, and is beneficial to all Americans. So what does a thoughtful

agenda for American immigration reform look like? Here are four guiding principles: Number one: We must respect the consent of the governed, that is the will of the people. Individuals who are not citizens do not have a right to American citizenship without the consent of the American people . . . Number two: We cannot compromise national security and public safety . . . Number three: Becoming a citizen means becoming an American. We must preserve patriotic assimilation . . . Number four: Our lawmakers must respect the rule of law and immigration is no exception. (The Heritage Foundation, 2021)

In the rest of this chapter, we provide a brief history of immigration policy in the United States followed by an analysis of how the Social Order and Social Justice perspectives on this topic are driven by different intuitions about: fairness and equality; freedom, choice, and responsibility; individual and group-based morality; and attitudes toward social change.

## A Brief History of Immigration Policy in the United States

From the founding of the country until about 1875, the United States had an open-door immigration policy. The Naturalization Act of 1790 allowed immigrants to acquire citizenship after a period of residence in the US, and there were no legal restrictions on the number of immigrants or on places of origin. From time to time, throughout the early to mid nineteenth century, serious opposition to immigration would arise – or at least opposition to immigrants from certain countries. The opposition was sometimes quite vehement, resulting in mob violence against certain groups, such as Irish Catholics in the 1850s (Cohn, 2000).

In the mid to late nineteenth century, there was growing opposition to immigration from China and Japan, as these immigrants were seen as undercutting the economic prospects of natives. As with the Irish, racism undoubtedly played a role (Daniels, 2002; Martin and Midgley, 2003). Responding to this pressure, Congress passed the Immigration Act of 1882, which prohibited newcomers from China, and later limited immigration from Japan.

By the end of the nineteenth century, when immigration from southern and eastern Europe was high, there was considerable debate about the optimal number of immigrants entering the United States. The Immigration Act of 1921 was the first law to set quotas for immigrants from eastern Europe and to put a ceiling on the overall number of immigrants allowed to enter the United States from all countries. This was followed by the even tougher Immigration Act of 1924, which banned immigration from Asia and set additional quotas on immigration from the eastern hemisphere. Levels of immigration plummeted after these legislative acts, and remained low for the next few decades (Daniels, 2002).

Immigration policy generally became less restrictive during and after World War II. The national mood shifted so that many Americans felt more effort should be made to bring policies in line with the American ideal of equality of opportunity.

At the height of the Civil Rights movement, another momentous piece of immigration legislation was passed – the 1965 Amendments to the Immigration and Nationality Act, also known as the Hart-Celler Act. This Act did away with the discriminatory national quota system and replaced it with the system that we have today. The current policy does not discriminate by country of origin and puts greater weight on immigrant

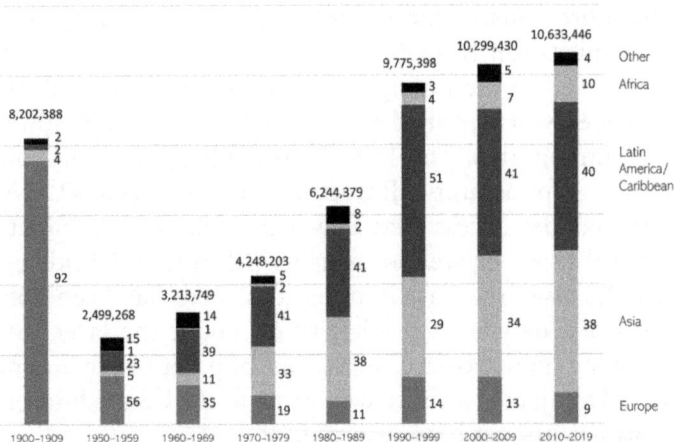

**Figure 6.1** Annual number of legal US immigrants by decade and percent of immigrants by region of origin, 1900–2019

*Source:* Data from US Department of Homeland Security, 2022

skills and family reunification (Daniels, 2002; Martin and Midgley, 2003).

Since the passing of the Hart-Celler Act, the number of immigrants entering the US has increased, especially from Latin America and Asia, though also from Africa and the Middle East, thus increasing racial and ethnic diversity in the United States (Iceland, 2017). These trends in immigration by global region of origin are illustrated in Figure 6.1. The figure shows that, whereas 92 percent of immigrants in the 1900–1909 period were from Europe, by 2010–2019 only 9 percent were. In 2010–2019, 40 percent of immigrants came from Latin America and the Caribbean, another 38 percent from Asia, and 10 percent from Africa.

While there have been a variety of policy debates over immigration since the 1965 legislation, changes to immigration policy have been relatively minor. Among the more consequential ones, the growth of unauthorized migration from Mexico in the post-World War II period led to the Immigration Reform and Control Act of 1986, which granted amnesty to 2.7 million unauthorized immigrants. The 1996 Personal Responsibility and Work Opportunity Reconciliation Act (PRWORA) reduced the access that new legal immigrants had to several types of welfare benefits (Martin and Midgley, 2003). Over the past two decades there has been considerable debate over what to do about the large and growing unauthorized immigrant population, including the "Dreamers" – those who came to the US as children. This has not yet been resolved.

Throughout history, Social Order and Social Justice perspectives have played a central role in debates about immigration. Those from the Social Order perspective typically have been concerned about high levels of immigration and the extent to which immigrants can successfully be assimilated into US society. Henry Cabot Lodge, a historian and long-time Massachusetts Senator, wrote in 1891 about the recent surge in immigrants from Italy, Russia, Hungary, and Poland. He proposed a literacy test for immigrants, believing it would preserve the American economy and character:

> We have the right to exclude illiterate persons from our immigration, and this test, combined with the others of a more general character, would in probability shut out a large part of the undesirable portion of the present immigration. It would reduce in a discriminating manner the total number of immigrants, and would thereby greatly benefit the labor market and help to maintain the rate of American wages. At the same time it would sift the immigrants who come to this country, and would shut out in a very large measure those elements which tend to lower the quality of American citizenship, and

which now in any cases gather in dangerous masses in the slums of our great cities. (Lodge, 1891: 36)

Conversely, the passage of the Hart-Celler Act in 1965 reflected the dominant Social Justice mood of the Civil Rights era. As a *New York Times* editorial from that year contended:

This country's immigration law, based upon racially angled national origins quotas, makes a strange counter-point to its progressive laws against racial discrimination at home. Immigration nowadays largely serves the humanitarian purpose of helping refugees and reunit-ing separated families. For this purpose the rigid quotas frozen into the law more than forty years ago have proved unworkable. (The New York Times, 1965)

Disagreements about immigration between those with a Social Justice perspective and those with a Social Order perspective, both historically and currently, have been shaped by factors other than racism or political expedience. Moral and philosophical concerns have also played an important role. We review these concerns below.

### Fairness and Equality

As we have seen, the Social Justice perspective defines fairness as achieving equality of outcomes across groups. With regards to immigration, this means open-ing our borders to immigrants seeking to improve their lives by taking part in the US economy and providing them with assistance, if needed, to make ends meet once here.

For instance, in 2015, during the Syrian civil war, those from the Social Justice perspective argued that the

United States was admitting too few refugees. They saw this as deeply unfair. In petitioning the Obama administration to increase the number of refugees, Senators Dick Durbin and Amy Klobuchar wrote:

> As the Syrian conflict enters its 5th year with no end in sight, we respectfully request that your Administration take action to significantly increase the number of Syrian refugees who are resettled in the United States. Our nation's founders came to our shores to escape religious persecution and the United States has a long tradition of providing safe haven to refugees. The United States traditionally accepts at least 50 percent of resettlement cases from the UN High Commissioner for Refugees (UNHCR). However, we have accepted only approximately 700 refugees since the beginning of the Syrian conflict, an unacceptably low number . . . We commend those countries that have committed to accepting a significant number of Syrian refugees relative to their population, including Australia, Canada, Finland, Germany, Norway, Sweden, and Switzerland. (Durbin and Klobuchar, 2015)

Those from the Social Justice perspective also often argue that immigrants, including unauthorized immigrants, should be eligible to receive more government assistance. Under current regulations, only refugees and immigrants with legal permanent residency who have lived in the US for at least five years have access to many types of programs, such as food assistance and Medicaid. From the Social Justice perspective, denying these kinds of benefits to immigrants who don't qualify is fundamentally unfair because doing so increases unequal outcomes and is from this perspective morally objectionable. As a 2020 Health Affairs blog post authored by a group of instructors and students at Harvard argues:

Unauthorized immigrants, who are usually of Hispanic descent, have a one in four chance of being food insecure ... Leaving anyone without adequate food is itself a horrifying human rights violation and counters the globally acknowledged right to food. Furthermore, if not supported in fulfilling their basic needs, unauthorized immigrants likely will disproportionately suffer from COVID-19 and hamper public health efforts to contain the virus ... The following policy recommendations can help meet the basic food security needs of all people currently in this country, including unauthorized immigrants, to alleviate hunger and ill health in the US. (Velasquez et al., 2020)

Those from the Social Order perspective usually see the system's role in applying rules and laws impartially as more important than a possible role as an equalizer of outcomes. This is one of the reasons why those from this perspective are particularly troubled by *unauthorized* immigration, as unauthorized migrants are by definition not following the rules for lawful entry. They are more likely to see such immigrants as jumping the queue, while those who follow the rules often face long wait times to receive permission to migrate legally.

Because of these different perspectives, there has been a long-running debate about what to do about the 11 million unauthorized immigrants already in the United States (Lopez et al., 2021). Social Justice proponents argue that they should be granted "amnesty" – a path to citizenship – as occurred under the 1986 legislation. Social Order proponents counter that granting amnesty would be unfair to those who have already waited for long periods and gone through proper channels. As immigrant policy analyst Pawel Styrna, writing for the Federation for American Immigration Reform, an organization that seeks lower levels of immigration, argued:

Amnesty is unfair to legal immigrants. It is understandable that people from all over the world wish to settle in the United States, but that makes it all the more necessary that they do so legally. Each year, over one million people are granted Legal Permanent Residency ("green cards"). They endure a costly, complicated, and long process that is necessary to maintain order and proper vetting. Thus, granting amnesty (regardless of the conditions) to people who violated our laws and effectively cut in line to get here is deeply unfair to those who followed the rules, respected our laws, and waited in line. (Styrna, 2021)

Many Social Order proponents further argue that because unauthorized immigrants have broken the law by entering the country, they should not have equal access to the benefits of citizenship, including access to government programs. As philosophy professor William F. Vallicella asserts:

Liberals believe in a vast panoply of social services provided by government and thus funded by taxation. But the quality of these services must degrade as the number of people who demand them rises. To take but one example, laws requiring hospitals to treat those in dire need whether or not they have a means of paying are reasonable and humane – or at least that can be argued with some show of plausibility. But such laws are reasonably enacted and reasonably enforced only in a context of social order. Without border control, not only will the burden placed on hospitals become unbearable, but the justification for the federal government's imposition of these laws on hospitals will evaporate. (Vallicella, 2021)

## *Freedom, Choice, and Responsibility*

The person with a Social Justice perspective often measures freedom in terms of one's ability to exercise power and influence. Because immigrants often have little power and influence, they are, from this perspective, viewed as having few choices and bearing little to no responsibility for their disadvantaged circumstances. They thus deserve support. Perhaps the best example of this are refugees who are admitted to the US for humanitarian reasons, including political persecution in their home countries. Immigrants who come for economic reasons, although they might not be fleeing political persecution, may be trying to avoid poverty and improve their economic well-being. Social Justice proponents see them as fellow human beings caught in a quandary not of their own making.

"Dreamers" make up one such group. Those from the Social Justice perspective highlight how Dreamers lack basic citizenship rights through no fault of their own because many were brought to the United States as children by their unauthorized immigrant parents. One sympathetic news story described how several beneficiaries of the Deferred Action for Childhood Arrivals (DACA) program – which allows Dreamers to avoid deportation for a renewable two-year period and become eligible for a work permit – met with President Joe Biden to press their plight:

> President Joe Biden met with six recipients of the Deferred Action for Childhood Arrivals program at the White House, where the young people expressed the urgent need for permanent protections for all undocumented immigrants. DACA recipient Maria Praeli said in a statement after the meeting that she was "enormously

grateful" that Biden listened to their stories of how their families have "struggled with the broken immigration system." "We were able to be candid with the president," Praeli said of herself and the other DACA recipients, often referred to as "Dreamers," who were brought to the U.S. as children. They detailed how "painful" it is to have one's immigration status "in limbo," Praeli said, adding that the meeting with Biden "made even clearer the incredibly high stakes of permanently protecting immigrants from deportation." (Ruiz-Grossman, 2021)

In contrast, those from the Social Order perspective focus less on immigrants who fall in the "Dreamer" category, and more on unauthorized immigrants who made the choice to enter the US illegally. Because of this illegal choice, they are generally seen as not deserving of special accommodations (von Spakovsky, 2018). Thus, those from the Social Order perspective emphasize how, ultimately, unauthorized immigrants are responsible for not having the rights that accompany citizenship. As Ronald W. Mortensen, writing for the Center for Immigration Studies (an organization committed to reducing immigration and effectively integrating legal immigrants), argued:

Illegal aliens commit criminal misdemeanors when they sneak into the United States. They teach their children to lie in order to hide their illegal status. They quickly graduate to felonies. They may use fraudulently obtained passports with fabricated visas. They illegally obtain Social Security cards. They criminally alter and forge documents. They perjure themselves on I-9 forms and obtain driver's licenses through deception. They recruit their friends to help them further their life of lies and deception and they put their employers in the position of knowingly hiring and harboring illegal aliens ... Legal immigration is people who accept personal responsibility and do not blame others for difficulties they face because of the bad choices that they and others made. Illegal immigration is people blaming others for the bad choices that they and their parents made and then demanding that they be granted special privileges not available to legal immigrants or American citizens, including total amnesty from serious felonies. (Mortensen, 2012)

As can be seen from the arguments above, proponents of Social Order and Social Justice often use different terminology when arguing their positions. Those from the Social Justice perspective use terms like "undocumented" or "unauthorized immigrants" and "Dreamers". Meanwhile, those from the Social Order perspective use terms like "illegal immigrants" or "illegal aliens" as a way to highlight the criminal aspect and to argue that such immigrants do not rightfully deserve US citizenship or support. The two groups' differing views on the degree to which non-legal immigrants should be held responsible for their situation drive these language choices.

More generally, Americans are split on the issue of illegal immigration. A 2021 poll showed that about 30 percent believed that unauthorized immigrants should not be allowed to stay in the country and another 26 percent believed that they should be eligible for permanent residency, but not US citizenship. A plurality, 42 percent, believed they should be eligible for citizenship (Pew Research Center, 2021a).

### *Individual and Group-Based Morality*

The Social Justice perspective emphasizes individual-based morality aimed at protecting the vulnerable. Today, those from this perspective overwhelmingly support generous immigration policies that would allow immigrants – legal or not – to lead better lives in America. This position reflects the famous inscription on the pedestal of the Statue of Liberty, which proclaims (from the 1883 poem by Emma Lazarus): "Give me your tired, your poor, Your huddled masses yearning to breathe free, The wretched refuse of your teeming shore. Send these, the homeless, tempest-tost to me, I lift my lamp beside the golden door!"

Today, an important component of immigration policy in many Western countries is the provision of refugee and humanitarian assistance, consistent with the goals of the Social Justice perspective. That is not to say that the Social Order perspective is indifferent to humanitarian aid, but they may differ in the extent to which they see the host country's government as responsible for providing such relief. As the US Department of State webpage stated at the time of this writing:

> The United States is the largest single provider of humanitarian assistance worldwide ... The primary goal of U.S. humanitarian assistance is to save lives and alleviate suffering by ensuring that vulnerable and crisis-affected individuals receive assistance and protection. U.S. funding provides life-saving assistance to tens of millions of displaced and crisis-affected people, including refugees, worldwide. Our assistance provides urgent, life-saving support, including food, shelter, safe drinking water, improved sanitation and hygiene, emergency healthcare services, child protection programs, and education, among other activities. (US Department of State, 2022)

Some from the Social Justice perspective see this commitment as necessary but not sufficient when it comes to our duty to help others. They believe we have an ethical obligation to open our borders to all people who want to enter. According to this view, there is no reason to prioritize the life of an American over the life of any other. As political science professor Chandran Kukathas puts it:

> [One] reason for favoring open borders is a principle of humanity. The great majority of the people of the world live in poverty, and for a significant number of them the most promising way of improving their condition is to move ... To say to such people that they are forbidden to cross a border in order to improve their condition is to say to them that it is justified that they be denied the opportunity to get out of poverty, or even destitution. (Kukathas, 2004: 380)

In contrast, the Social Order perspective holds that while the well-being of would-be migrants is important, it should be weighed against the potential costs to the host society of admitting and supporting them. Objections to generous immigration policies are thus often raised on several grounds, including concerns over the potential negative impact of immigration on jobs and wages, costly fiscal impacts, reduced security and increased crime, and lower social cohesion. Regarding security, for instance, the Heritage Foundation asserts:

> Every nation has the right, recognized by both international and domestic law, to secure its borders and ports of entry and control what and who is coming into its country. A disorganized and chaotic immigration system encourages people to go around the law and is a clear invitation to those who wish to take advantage of our openness to harm the nation. Secure borders, especially in a time of terrorist threat, are crucial to American national security. (The Heritage Foundation, 2021)

There has been a lot of research on the effects of immigration in the US. With respect to immigration's effects on jobs and wages, a key question has been whether immigrants complement the existing workforce by doing jobs that Americans otherwise couldn't or wouldn't do, or whether they take jobs from native-born workers. Different study designs have yielded different answers. Harvard economist George Borjas found immigration had a moderate negative impact on the wages of low-skilled workers (Borjas, 2017). However, a National Academies report summarizing many different studies concluded that negative effects on wages are small and limited to prior immigrants and the native-born high school dropouts who compete with them most directly for jobs (National Academies, 2017). The debate is not yet settled.

The broad fiscal effects of immigration are similarly difficult to measure, as a comprehensive estimate has to take into account the amount of taxes immigrants pay versus the services they consume – numbers that are often difficult to come by. The National Academies report referenced above concluded that the overall fiscal impact of immigration at the federal level is positive over the long run, especially when one considers the fiscal contributions of the children of immigrants as they age and pay more taxes. However, there can be negative effects at the local and state level, largely due to the costs of educating the children of immigrants. The report also concluded that immigration has a positive long-run impact on economic growth in the United States (National Academies, 2017). For instance, immigrants have played an important role in the growth and innovation of the tech industry in Silicon Valley.

Regarding the impact of immigration on crime, a recent review of a large number of studies concluded that there is a small and weak negative association between the two (i.e., more immigration in an area is associated with somewhat lower levels of crime). The review also found significant variation across studies and that a definitive assessment of the nature of the association is complicated due to the often low quality of official crime data and the likely under-reporting of crimes by unauthorized immigrants (Ousey and Kubrin, 2018). While it is possible to point to startling examples of migrant crime – for instance, the Central American gang MS-13 – the authors argue that immigrants typically come to the US for a better life. They usually seek employment opportunities or to reunite with family members, and are thus less likely to commit crimes than the native-born with a similar socioeconomic profile (Pendergast et al., 2018; Sampson, 2008).

Regarding the impact of immigration on social cohesion, and consistent with a Social Order perspective, an influential study by political scientist Robert Putnam found that cohesion was lower in more diverse communities, at least in the short run. He speculated that in highly diverse communities people of all races tend to "hunker down," leading to lower levels of trust (even in one's own group), altruism, and community cooperation. The study also found that people living in highly diverse communities report fewer friends (Putnam, 2007). Despite this finding, Putnam ends his article on an optimistic note by suggesting that the fragmentation resulting from diversity might be temporary. He highlights successful examples of diversity not leading to division, such as in the US military, certain religious institutions, and with prior waves of immigrants (Putnam, 2007).

Those from the Social Order and Social Justice perspectives also tend to have different views on a related issue: the extent to which we should adopt approaches that foster immigrant assimilation versus those that promote multiculturalism. Those who favor a Social Justice perspective are more likely to favor a multicultural approach to immigration, which means respecting and sometimes nurturing individual and group-level cultural differences. According to this perspective, applying pressure to assimilate presupposes that one culture is superior to another, and this can result in the stigmatization of already-marginalized individuals. In a *Toronto Star* editorial, writer and theatrical producer Louis MacPherson contends:

> Multiculturalism is important because it dilutes and dissipates the divisiveness of ignorance. It is important because it encourages dialogue, often between radically different cultures that have radically different perspectives. It is important because it softens the indifference of tolerance, and embraces it with the genuine humanity of acceptance. It is a bridge between the divide of tolerance and acceptance ... We should cherish the opportunity to sublimate the notion of a rigid Western, Eastern, Christian, Judaic, Islamic, etc. viewpoint and encourage people instead to look at society and culture from the viewpoint of a globally infused diaspora. A little nationalism, like a little knowledge, can be a very dangerous thing and, as history has shown to the point of redundancy, it can be a catalyst for egregiously barbaric and immoral treatment. (MacPherson, 2007)

In contrast, those from the Social Order perspective contend that assimilation is crucial for social cohesion. Without social cohesion, ethnic divisions will make long-term coexistence and cooperation less likely. Many multicultural nations have unsuccessfully struggled to avoid division and strife, such as the former Yugoslavia (with a mixed population of Serbs, Croats, Bosnians, and others) and Rwanda (Tutsis and Hutus). Even though the United States has a different history than these nations, and has long been a country of immigrants, those from the Social Order perspective argue that assimilation was a key factor in explaining the

US's past successes. As Howard Husock, a contributing editor to the *City Journal*, argued in a commentary titled "Bring Back Assimilation":

> Most of the debate over immigration has focused on whom we admit and why, and why our border control is so ineffective . . . It is a mistake, though, to think that Americans are more worried about who has a green card than they are about immigrant assimilation, a less discussed matter. The idea that immigrants should, and can, become Americans has been a powerful one, a reflection of the fact that ours is a society based on values and laws, rather than a single faith and a common blood. Lately, discussing immigrant assimilation has become less than acceptable in polite company out of a concern that assimilation imposes Anglo-Saxon Protestant culture on others. But the majority thinks that newcomers should learn English, which is endorsed by 87% of Americans in one Rasmussen survey, and become American citizens. This makes clear that, notwithstanding the affection for multiculturalism among elites, average Americans still believe in the melting pot. (Husock, 2008)

In short, Social Justice proponents generally argue that permissive immigration policies are necessary to prevent harm and enhance well-being among individuals who, for one reason or another, seek a better life in the US. They also argue that immigration brings benefits for society, such as economic innovation and growth. However, this argument tends to be secondary to their focus on our moral obligation to do the right thing for individuals in need. It is in this sense that the morality of those with a Social Justice perspective can be considered individual-based, that is, deeply rooted in a concern for the well-being of vulnerable individuals.

In contrast, those from the Social Order perspective tend to worry about the costs of immigration to society, including its effect on social cohesion and, in the localities most affected, budgetary overruns and crime. People with a Social Order perspective seek to balance the desire of individual immigrants to pursue a better life against the responsibility of the host society to ensure that its own citizens' needs and interests are taken care of. It is in this sense that the morality of those with a Social Order perspective is considered group-based, that is, deeply rooted in a concern for the order and stability of society as a whole.

### Social Change

Individuals from the Social Justice perspective believe we need to adopt policies that reduce individual suffering and that policymakers have the moral capacity and skill to successfully manage social change. This belief generally leads them to support allowing more immigrants, including refugees, to enter the US. This approach was reflected in German Chancellor Angela Merkel's "Wir schaffen das" – or "We will manage" – defense of her decision to allow a large number of refugees from Syria and other countries to enter Germany in 2015 (Delcker, 2015).

In the US, those from the Social Justice perspective tend to endorse social change policies consistent with what they see as a moral imperative, including providing Dreamers a path to citizenship, raising the ceiling on the number of refugees admitted, providing more generous welfare benefits to immigrants, and allowing immigrants and refugees detained at the US-Mexico border easier entrance into the United States. From the Social Justice perspective, as long as people are suffering, we have an obligation to move swiftly to develop policies to help them. It is not surprising, therefore, that those from the

Social Justice perspective saw the Trump administration's restrictive immigration policies as antithetical to their own policy-change objectives. As Shelby Gonzales of the progressive Center on Budget and Policy Priorities wrote in welcoming a Biden administration's executive order reversing many of Trump's initiatives:

> The executive order directs federal agencies to "review" the harmful public charge rules from the Trump Administration, which basically serve as a wealth test for people who want to come to, or stay in, the United States. Those new rules made it hard for many people without substantial means who were already here to remain, and for many who sought legal entry to unite with their family members. The public charge rules and other harmful actions by the Trump Administration sowed fear among immigrants and their family members and, as a result, many are forgoing health coverage, nutrition assistance, and other services for which they are eligible. In the midst of the current health and economic crises, these benefits are vital to helping individuals and families survive, making swift action to reverse the Trump public charge rules critical. By reversing these harsh immigration policies, our nation will start to turn the page on this ugly chapter of anti-immigrant action, once again recognize the important role that immigrants play in our communities, and empower families to seek medical care and other supportive services without fear or delay. (Gonzales, 2021)

Proponents of Social Order, on the other hand, are often wary of policymakers' ability to engineer a more equitable and robust immigration policy without creating unintended negative consequences. Some from the Social Order perspective thus seek to minimize, or slow, social change by reducing immigration (Styrna, 2021) and/or stopping illegal immigration (The Heritage

Foundation, 2021). Other Social Order proponents cite concerns over assimilation and social cohesion or a combination of all of these factors (Center for Immigration Studies, 2021). For instance, many proponents of Social Order are concerned that amnesty or a path to citizenship will set up an incentive structure that leads to yet more illegal immigration. In this line of thinking, would-be unauthorized migrants become more likely to cross the border because they believe that they too might be able to gain citizenship someday. As Pawel Styrna argues:

> Amnesty encourages more illegal migration. The granting of mass amnesty impedes efforts to deter illegal immigration by making others think they can enter illegally and get an amnesty later. This is what happened after an amnesty was approved by Congress and signed into law by President Ronald Reagan in 1986. It stands as a case study in how good intentions can result in bad law ... Sen. Charles Grassley (R-Iowa), who was elected in 1980, emphasized during a debate on immigration reform in February 2013, that ". . . The American people were told that this would be a one-time shot. The incentive to buy-in to the argument was a promise of enforcement." Following the signing of the bill into law in 1986, 2.7 million illegal aliens were granted amnesty while approximately another 3 million unauthorized migrants remained. Today, there are at least 14.5 million, according to FAIR's [Federation for American Immigrant Reform] latest estimates. (Styrna, 2021)

While a more commonly accepted estimate of the number of unauthorized immigrants in the United States is 11 million (Lopez et al., 2021), the general argument that there are many more unauthorized immigrants in the United States today than when the amnesty bill was

Immigration

passed in 1986 holds. Thus, in an important way, the 1986 legislation did not work as intended and created more social change than those with a Social Order perspective see as desirable.

## *Conclusion*

How much legal immigration should a nation permit and how much illegal immigration should it tolerate? Should immigrants be expected to assimilate to American culture or should American culture change to accommodate immigrants' needs? How much responsibility should the US take for ensuring the well-being of unauthorized migrants and their children? Is it ever okay to say no to immigration or to prioritize the well-being of citizens?

Those with a Social Justice perspective often believe it is hypocritical for a "nation of immigrants" to prevent or limit immigration, especially when immigrants face squalid or oppressive conditions in their home countries. They argue we have a moral obligation to do whatever we can to end suffering and that we should be willing to make sacrifices to do so. To do otherwise is to reveal ourselves as selfish at best and, at worst, as bigoted.

Those with a Social Order perspective, in contrast, tend to argue that it is irresponsible for a nation of tax-paying citizens not to prevent or limit immigration unless allowing immigration is in the interests of the country. They see placing limits on immigration as a necessary and legitimate means of protecting citizens' interests. They argue that, while it is unfortunate that some immigrants face squalid or oppressive conditions in their home countries, the would-be host nation has a moral obligation to prioritize and protect the well-being of those legally authorized to live within its borders. To do otherwise is to reveal ourselves as impractical and short-sighted.

As we have shown throughout this chapter, the divergent views on immigration held by those with a Social Justice or Social Order perspective can best be understood as the product of divergent moral and ethical assumptions regarding fairness and equality; freedom, choice, and responsibility; individual and group-based morality; and attitudes toward social change. To formulate policies that properly balance the moral and philosophical insights of both sides, we need to develop better approaches to producing and consuming information about not just immigration, but all forms of inequality in society. In the next and final chapter of this book, we provide some ideas for achieving this balance.

# 7

# Where Do We Go from Here?

> In politics . . . it is almost a commonplace, that a party
> of order or stability, and a party of progress or reform,
> are both necessary elements of a healthy state of polit-
> ical life . . . Each of these modes of thinking derives its
> utility from the deficiencies of the other; but it is in a
> great measure the opposition of the other that keeps
> each within the limits of reason and sanity.
>
> John Stuart Mill, *On Liberty*

We wrote this book to show how the Social Order–Social
Justice framework is useful for understanding why contemporary Americans disagree about social inequality.
We began by describing the values, beliefs, and moral
intuitions associated with each perspective. We then
applied the framework to disagreements about social
problems that many of us would like to solve, including
gender inequality, racial and ethnic inequality, income
inequality, and immigration policy. We examined how
the values, beliefs, and moral intuitions contained within
the Social Order and Social Justice perspectives drive
disagreements about the causes of these problems and
the best policy approaches to solving them.

If our analysis is correct, then debates over whose
assumptions are "right" or "wrong" are bound to be

fruitless. People do not easily abandon their moral and philosophical principles. And even if they did, as John Stuart Mill argued over 150 years ago, permitting one perspective to dominate the other would bring us no closer to a solution, since each contains a wisdom the other lacks. Therefore, instead of spending time arguing with and villainizing those whose views differ from our own, as if reality were reducible to a single view, we need to improve our collective ability to balance insights from various perspectives.

Before continuing with our suggestions, we first address a potential criticism. Someone might reasonably point out that the Social Order and Social Justice perspectives share much in common with traditional conservative and liberal divides. While there is certainly some overlap, the two frameworks differ in important ways. For example, liberals and conservatives both tend to endorse the moral value of caring for the welfare of others, especially the vulnerable, but they tend to diverge when it comes to endorsing the moral value of caring for the order and stability of social systems (Graham et al., 2009). Similarly, people can endorse both Social Order and Social Justice principles, values, and beliefs to varying degrees.

When people care about both Social Order and Social Justice, their opinions about social issues will tend to diverge from the standard, polarized liberal and conservative narratives and align with a more moderate position. Indeed, our analysis leads us to speculate that political partisans are more likely to adopt either a Social Order or a Social Justice perspective in their more extreme forms. While the majority of Americans do not align with such extremes (Pew Research Center, 2021b), many activists, pundits, and social media "influencers" do (Smith et al., 2020). And since the latter groups exert a powerful influence over public discourse, understanding the underlying nature of their viewpoints and disagreements is essential for understanding why each side supports or rejects particular arguments and policy solutions.

Indeed, as demonstrated throughout this book, disagreements about the causes, consequences, and solutions to problems of inequality are not due to a lack of statistical data. Of course, more and better data is useful for crafting policy and helping settle disputes that arise over basic facts, like whether unauthorized immigrants commit more crime than others. However, more and better data alone will not motivate people with different perspectives to see evidence similarly, since it's often the *interpretation* of statistical patterns, rather than the patterns themselves, about which people disagree.

There are at least two reasons to expect statistical data to play only a limited role in dispute resolution. First, unlike in the natural sciences – where cause and effect are more easily established – establishing causal inference in the social sciences is notoriously difficult. For example, a program that provides cash transfers to single-parent families might reduce poverty in the short term but could have unwanted negative effects in the long term, such as undermining family formation or reducing incentives to work. Such downstream effects are difficult to measure using current social science methods, let alone link to a specific policy.

Second, as we have argued, disagreements over the interpretation of data tend to be rooted in moral and philosophical leanings that lead people not only to take different positions in response to the same data but also to view each other's positions as morally and philosophically bankrupt. It is for this reason that, despite the twenty-first century's unprecedented access to statistical data, disagreements over the causes, consequences, and solutions to problems of inequality remain rampant.

Simply asking people to be more objective, open-minded, or compassionate is unlikely to be effective when it comes to settling disputes. Human beings, whether scientists or members of the public, are motivated reasoners. We are better at marshaling arguments and evidence to support our pre-existing views than we are at systematically weighing and merging arguments and evidence derived from differing viewpoints. This is not to suggest that trying to become more open-minded has no value. Rather, it is to suggest that it would be naive to rely solely on our individual abilities and willingness to become more open-minded as the main way to make public discourse about inequality more productive.

### Toward More Constructive Disagreement

To find ways to disagree more productively on issues of inequality, we need to increase our reliance on what Jonathan Haidt and Greg Lukianoff (2018) call "institutionalized disconfirmation," and what Jonathan Rauch (2021) calls the "reality-based community." According to Haidt and Lukianoff, institutionalized disconfirmation is made possible by a system of deliberation in which individuals and groups understand and expect that their claims about the causes of and solutions to social problems *must be challenged*. This process of challenging claims is necessary to narrow the gap between reality and interpretation that inevitably emerges because of motivated reasoning. Challenging one another's interpretations reveals blind spots in our understanding of reality, thereby increasing the accuracy of our perspectives and the likely effectiveness of our proposed solutions.

According to Rauch, reality-based communities operate according to two basic principles. The first is the *fallibilist principle*, which states that "no one gets the final say" and everyone's assertions are provisional pending further analysis (Rauch 2021: 88). The second is the *empirical principle* which states that "no one has personal authority" to proclaim something is true unless that truth is obtainable by others using established methods of verification (89). Rauch explains that what matters most in a reality-based community is "not that individuals in the community be unbiased but that they have different biases, so that I see your mistakes and you see mine" (73). Without support from such a community, the accumulation of scientific knowledge in support of effective solutions to problems of inequality will remain elusive.

The Social Order–Social Justice framework describes the two main competing sides that must be brought into dialogue with one another if potential solutions to problems of inequality are to emerge. On one side are those who emphasize structural causes and constraints. On the other are those who emphasize behavioral choices and cultural practices. That both sides vie for supporters in public discourse is not itself a problem. The problem arises when one or both sides adopt a winner-take-all approach that requires rejecting the other side's insights. When this happens, our collective capacity to benefit from our opponent's challenges and to discern complex and contradictory causes and solutions recedes. And with it goes any hope of developing policy approaches based on a nuanced and careful understanding of the current state of the world. When public discourse deteriorates to the point it has today, it is easy to lose sight of the fact that *winning the argument* is not the same as *solving the problem*.

So how do we create a space for constructive engagement on issues of inequality? When we think about transforming public discourse on these topics, any potential path forward will require a shift either in the way information is produced and conveyed, or in how the public receives and interprets that information, or both.

## *Viewpoint Diversity in Media and Social Science*

The proliferation of divergent narratives accounting for the origins of inequality is linked in important ways to the fragmentation of today's news and social media markets into ideological niches. Given the decentralization of media, one possible path forward is to continue fostering what has come to be known as the "marketplace of ideas." This approach – which dominates today's news and social media – is grounded in traditional notions of freedom of speech. It allows many voices and arguments to be aired and, ideally over time, such airing should result in weak arguments being discarded and strong ones being retained. Transparency on the part of news and commentary outlets about their ideological commitments can facilitate this approach by allowing listeners to calibrate the biases of what they're hearing, seeing, or reading. But, even without such transparency, the biases of a particular outlet usually become known over time. For example, although it may not have been clear at the outset, at this point, people who watch Fox News typically know they are watching news from the political right, while those who watch MSNBC typically know they are watching news from the political left.

Despite the potential of the marketplace of ideas to enable a wide range of perspectives and conclusions to compete for public attention and acceptance, there are reasons to be skeptical of its ability to serve as a mechanism for yielding high-quality, trustworthy information about the world, at least in the short run. That skepticism largely stems from the incentives in place among most media outlets.

Rauch argues that digital media reward emotion-driven reporting over accuracy and precision because eliciting strong emotions draws more attention and thus more views and subscriptions. Supporting this idea, the authors of a 2018 study at the Massachusetts Institute of Technology found that falsehoods were 70% more likely to be retweeted than truth (Vosoughi et al., 2018). The authors speculated that the higher retweet rate was likely due to the greater capacity of false reports to elicit shock, outrage, and disgust. Rauch spells out the implications of this incentive structure when he argues that digital media reward "instantaneity and impulsivity," giving "new substance to the old saying that a lie circles the world before the truth gets its boots on" (2021: 133).

In addition to these challenges, the *social media* marketplace of ideas promotes and rewards ad hominem attacks, which are attacks on the person, rather than on the idea. Such attacks further fuel the emotion-driven tone of social media output. On top of this, social media enables anonymity, thus separating reporting from accountability. While both problems – ad hominem attacks and anonymity – do not apply to today's news media outlets, the problem of emotion-driven reporting does. It is thus fair to conclude that although the digitally mediated marketplace of ideas excels at promoting freedom of expression, relying on it as a strategy for generating high-quality, trustworthy information about the world is risky.

Generating high-quality, trustworthy news in a consistent fashion will likely require developing new processes to produce legitimate "news." With that in mind, one possible way forward is to adopt an institutionalized, rule-based approach to producing ideologically balanced, truth-focused news. This approach has been successful in other domains of public life. Classic examples include checks and balances among the separated powers of government and the peer review process in science, although as we suggest below the latter is in dire need of repair.

In the realm of government, the founding fathers were pragmatic idealists. They created a system that acknowledges and exploits the motivated reasoning and tribal proclivities of regular people. By requiring ideas to be publicly vetted, voted on, and subjected to review and veto by different government bodies, the founders engineered a system that works to transform disagreements into compromise. This is the genius of James Madison's statement in the Federalist Papers 51 that, "Ambition must be made to counteract ambition."

When it comes to knowledge creation, the system of checks and balances in the academic peer review process is highly effective, provided certain criteria are met. When a research paper is submitted to a journal, the editor sends it out to experts in the field who provide "blind" (anonymous) feedback and typically make recommendations for what needs to be improved before the research paper warrants publication. The authors then must revise their work based on the reviewers' feedback. When done properly, the academic peer review process ensures that scientific "findings" have been properly vetted before becoming available to other scientists and the public.

The peer review process only works properly, however, when people with a *diversity of opinions* review one another's work. Whether in academic research or news reporting, humans are motivated reasoners who are more inclined to find fault with works whose findings or conclusions they disagree with. Again, this in and of itself is not a problem provided that the review

162

process exposes scientific works to criticism from multiple ideological perspectives prior to publication. If, however, participants and peer reviewers all share the same ideological commitments, collective blind spots are sure to arise, and the output produced is likely to be less reality-based than it otherwise could be.

A troubling trend in recent years is that viewpoint *uniformity* in both the academic peer review process and the production of news is on the rise. Studies show a growing political imbalance among university faculty, with a low and declining proportion identifying as conservative and a high and increasing proportion identifying as liberal (Abrams, 2016). News media suffer from a similar increasing skewness (Kuypers, 2014). For instance, a 2020 study of journalists found that 80 percent lean politically to the left (Hassell et al., 2020). Under such conditions, works whose conclusions or positions contradict the shared ideology of the left would receive more rigorous critique from peer reviewers than those that support it. When this happens, the review process becomes incapable of producing a balanced critique, regardless of how well it adheres to its own procedures.

We believe a checks and balances approach akin to those used in reviewing scientific works could, in principle, be adopted by the various news media. This would not replace the free exchange of ideas, but rather add a new safeguard. In this model, a news media organization would rely on a system where journalists with different ideological perspectives review one another's work prior to publication. Were such an approach embraced, the now blurry line between social media output and legitimate news may become more distinct, enabling the public to better differentiate between ideologically driven opinion and reality-based, truth-focused information, and to choose which they prefer to consume.

Adopting such a system would be transformational in the world of media. The trajectory of today's news vendors, however, is moving in the opposite direction. Instead of governing themselves according to an internal process where journalists with different perspectives collaborate in framing the news, news vendors have shifted toward a strategy of cultivating loyal audiences eager to see their preferred narrative favored and alternative narratives disparaged. Such pandering has led to the amplification of extreme viewpoints at the expense of more moderate or nuanced ones. One result is that the news-consuming public has come to believe it lives in a more caustic, closed-minded, and argumentative world than it actually does. This leads people to view with suspicion and derision those whose views differ from their own, thereby weakening the foundation necessary for productive public discourse and problem solving.

It should be noted that by emphasizing the importance of reviewing scientific results and news stories from different perspectives, we are not arguing that the "truth," if we could ever definitively discern it, is always at the midpoint between conflicting claims. In some instances, the Social Justice or the Social Order perspective might have stronger claims on the truth. What we do argue, however, is that the process of considering alternative viewpoints is essential for allowing a full vetting of information and evidence to occur so that our understanding of the world can be brought into greater alignment with how the world actually is.

In addition to emphasizing viewpoint diversity in the *production* of social science knowledge and news we believe it is essential to emphasize viewpoint diversity in preparing citizens to become *educated consumers* of such information. The latter can best be achieved by focusing on education.

## *Viewpoint Diversity in Education*

When it comes to changing how we *consume* information, arguably the most important mechanism is education. The path to change in this sector requires redefining how teachers are trained and how they understand their jobs in the classroom. To appreciate different ideological perspectives, teachers should be prepared and encouraged to explore a wide range of viewpoints with their students. There may be more than one way to accomplish this goal.

One way is to ask educators – and the institutions they work within – to avoid taking sides in the curricula they teach. The classroom would be a space to explore, but not draw conclusions about, inequality and other aspects of the social world. This would require teachers to avoid taking ideological stances and instead present students with a diversity of viewpoints *as if all were on equal moral footing with one another*. The goal would be to teach students to grasp the moral and philosophical underpinnings of different perspectives and to choose for themselves which, if any, they find compelling. Using this approach, students would learn to recognize the underlying moral and philosophical commitments of those with whom they agree or disagree, perhaps making them better able to engage in disagreements without villainizing the other side, or better able to serve as moderators or peacemakers when disagreements arise.

Taking it a step further, educators could explicitly recognize that different ideological perspectives often shape conclusions in a way that is independent of facts, drawing on history and current events for concrete examples of how this occurs. This would encourage students to think critically about the information they encounter by teaching them to identify, where appropriate, its ideological framing.

Of course, not all viewpoints warrant equal emphasis in an educational setting. Especially in K-12 schools, drawing lines around such content is standard practice, such as when school boards approve curricula. One of the questions such practices raise, however, is whether certain viewpoints or questions should be omitted because they lack evidence or are deemed offensive or potentially dangerous to the target audience. In such instances, institutions should, at a minimum, ensure that a diversity of viewpoints is reflected in the decision-making process and that the criteria used to include or exclude content are clearly articulated.

A second model, albeit a less desirable one, is to relax the expectation that teachers present multiple perspectives and simply ask them to be clear about which perspective they (and their institutions) are teaching from. In this version, teachers would be free to present information in a balanced or unbalanced manner, as they (and their institutions) see fit. However, in so doing, they would make clear to students, using age-appropriate language, which assumptions underpin the ideological positions they (and their institutions) are taking. Teachers might also spend time discussing the assumptions of perspectives they are *not* giving voice to so that students are made aware that other approaches exist. Students could then explore these other perspectives outside of the school setting if they wish.

Ultimately, by implementing either of these two approaches – but especially the first one – students would emerge from their educational experience with a fuller understanding of the range of morally valid ways of approaching discussions of inequality and other aspects of the social world. In the medium and long term, such an approach could fundamentally reshape how the public consumes and interprets information. It might also increase the public's demand for civility when policy interventions are publicly debated and discussed.

Our experience writing this book has led us to believe that adopting a "viewpoint diversity" approach to media and education would improve our collective ability to discuss and solve problems of inequality in society. The vetting approach implied by the viewpoint diversity model would transform the production and presentation of news and ensure the publication of ideologically balanced social science research. Shifting our educational system toward recognizing viewpoint diversity would improve how news and social science output is consumed and interpreted by the public.

These are not the only institutions capable of creating a space for constructive engagement on issues of inequality, however. There are some state legislatures, for example, which are dominated by people who hold a Social Order perspective and therefore have difficulty incorporating multiple viewpoints. Our focus on media and education is based on the fact that they are in the information production and dissemination business and that one of their fundamental goals is to provide trustworthy information about our social world that can be used to make sound decisions. If institutions such as these do not embrace viewpoint diversity, they are bound to fall short of this goal.

Social *in*justice and social *dis*order are perennial threats to society that manifest in a wide range of social problems. To solve such problems, social policies are needed that honor the assumptions and concerns of both the Social Justice and Social Order perspectives. Before such policies can be formulated, however, a clearer understanding of the nature of the disagreement between the two perspectives is needed. Our aim has been to provide such an understanding. We measure our success by the extent to which the reader is better able to identify the underlying assumptions of and see value in the perspectives articulated by both sides.

# References

Abrams, S. (2016). Professors moved left since 1990s, rest of country did not. *Heterdox Academy: The Blog.* https://heterodoxacademy.org/blog/professors-moved-left-but-country-did-not

Ahn, H. (2018). Affirmative action: An unfair means of discrimination. *The Cornell Review*, October 31.

Alexander, M. (2020). America, this is your chance. *The New York Times*, June 26.

American Psychological Association (2005). Men and women: No big difference. *Research in Action.* https://www.apa.org/research/action/difference

Arcidiacono, P., Aucejo, E. M., Fang, H., and Spenner, K. I. (2011). Does affirmative action lead to mismatch? A new test and evidence. *Quantitative Economics*, 2(3), 303–333. https://doi.org/10.3982/qe83

Arcidiacono, P., and Lovenheim, M. (2016). Affirmative action and the quality-fit trade-off. *Journal of Economic Literature*, 54(1), 3–51.

Association of American Medical Colleges (2017). 2017 Applicant and matriculant data tables (December). https://aamc-black.global.ssl.fastly.net/production/media/filer_public/5c/26/5c262575-52f9-4608-96d6-a78cdaa4b203/2017_applicant_and_matriculant_data_tables.pdf

Auten, G., and Splinter, D. (2019). Income inequality in the

# References

United States: Using tax data to measure long-term trends. Working Paper, 1–43. www.davidsplinter.com

Balcerowicz, L., and Radzikowski, M. (2018). The case for a targeted criticism of the welfare state. *Cato Journal*, *38*(1), 1–16. https://www.cato.org/cato-journal/winter-2018/case-targeted-criticism-welfare-state#references

Batko, S., Oneto, A. D., and Shroyer, A. (2020). Unsheltered homelessness. Urban Institute, December 3. https://www.urban.org/research/publication/unsheltered-homelessness-trends-characteristics-and-homeless-histories

Batlova, J., Hanna, M., and Levesque, C. (2021). Frequently requested statistics on immigrants and immigration in the United States. https://www.migrationpolicy.org/article/frequently-requested-statistics-immigrants-and-immigration-united-states-2020#immig-now-historical

Beckett, L. (2020). At least 25 Americans were killed during protests and political unrest in 2020. *The Guardian*, October 31.

Berman, Y. (2018). The long run evolution of absolute intergenerational mobility. Stone Center on Socio-Economic Inequality, October 19. https://doi.org/10.2139/ssrn.3269831

Bernhardt, A., Morris, M., and Handcock, M. S. (1995). Women's gains or men's losses? A closer look at the shrinking gender gap in earnings. *American Journal of Sociology*, *101*(2), 302–328.

Blau, F. D., and Kahn, L. M. (2017). The gender wage gap. *Journal of Economic Literature*, *55*(3), 789–865. https://doi.org/10.2307/j.ctt1tm7gsm.15

Boghossian, P. (2020). The illiberalism of social justice. *New Discourses*, February 25. https://newdiscourses.com/2020/02/illiberalism-social-justice

Borjas, G. J. (2017). The wage impact of the Marielitos: A reappraisal. *ILR Review*, *70*(5), 1077–1110. https://doi.org/10.1177/0019793917692945

Bowen, W. G., Bok, D., and Burkhart, G. (1999). A report

card on diversity: Lessons for business from higher education. *Harvard Business Review*, 77(1), 138–149.

Burstein, P. (2007). Jewish educational and economic success in the United States: A search for explanations. *Sociological Perspectives*, 50(2), 209–228. https://doi.org/10.1525/sop.2007.50.2.209

Butler, J. (1999). *Gender Trouble*, 2nd edition. New York: Routledge.

Caldwell, C. (2020). *The Age of Entitlement: America Since the Sixties*. Simon and Schuster.

Calzada, E., and Hough, C. (2021). Critical race theory needs to be in our schools. University of Texas at Austin, UT News. https://news.utexas.edu/2021/05/25/critical-race-theory-needs-to-be-in-our-schools

Carnevale, A. P., and Smith, N. (2014). Gender discrimination is at the heart of the wage gap. *Time*, May 19. https://time.com/105292/gender-wage-gap

Center for Immigration Studies (2021). About the Center for Immigration Studies. https://cis.org/Center-For-Immigration-Studies-Background

Charen, M. (2018). What the Times misses about poverty. *National Review*, September 14. https://www.nationalreview.com/2018/09/new-york-times-story-misunderstands-poverty

Charles, M., and Grusky, D. B. (2005). *Occupational Ghettos: The Worldwide Segregation of Women and Men*. Stanford University Press.

Chetty, R., Hendren, N., Kline, P., Saez, E., and Turner, N. (2014). Is the United States still a land of opportunity? Recent trends in intergenerational mobility. *American Economic Review*, 104(5), 141–147. https://doi.org/10.1257/aer.104.5.141

Christian, C. M., and Bennett, S. (1998). *Black Saga: The African American Experience: A Chronology*. Basic Civitas Books.

Cohn, R. L. (2000). Nativism and the end of the mass

migration of the 1840s and 1850s. *Journal of Economic History*, *60*(2), 361–383. https://doi.org/10.1017/s002205 0700025134

Corak, M., Lindquist, M. J., and Mazumder, B. (2014). A comparison of upward and downward intergenerational mobility in Canada, Sweden and the United States. *Labour Economics*, *30*, 185–200. https://doi.org/10.1016/j.labeco .2014.03.013

Costa, D. L. (2000). From mill town to board room: The rise of women's paid labor. *Journal of Economic Perspectives*, *14*(4), 101–122. https://doi.org/10.1257/jep.14.4.101

Daniels, R. (2002). *Coming to America*, 2nd edition. Perrennial.

Delcker, J. (2015). Merkel on migration: "We will manage." *Politico*, October 8. https://www.politico.eu/article/merkel -on-migration-we-will-manage

Delgado, R., and Stefancic, J. (2001). *Critical Race Theory: An Introduction*. New York University Press.

Desmond, M. (2018). Americans want to believe jobs are the solution to poverty. They're not. *The New York Times*, September 11.

Downey, D. (2008). Black/white differences in school per-formance: The oppositional culture explanation. *Annual Review of Sociology*, *34*, 107–126.

Durbin, D., and Klobuchar, A. (2015). Senators urge President to allow more Syrian refugees to resettle in U.S. https:// www.durbin.senate.gov/newsroom/press-releases/senators -urge-president-to-allow-more-syrian-refugees-to-resettle -in-us

Edin, K. J., and Shaefer, H. L. (2015). *$2.00 a Day: Living on Almost Nothing in America*. Mariner Books.

England, P., and Li, S. (2006). Desegregation stalled: The changing gender composition of college majors, 1971–2002. *Gender and Society*, *20*(5), 657–677. https://doi.org /10.1177/0891243206290753

Erwin, E. L. (2012). Evangelical equality: The feminism of

# References

Phyllis Schlafly. Lehigh University, Theses and Dissertations. Paper 1186. https://core.ac.uk/download/pdf/228641177 .pdf

Espenshade, T. J., and Radford, A. (2009). *No Longer Separate, Not Yet Equal: Race and Class in Elite College Admission and Campus Life.* Princeton University Press.

Fang, B. (2019). Why affirmative action is racist and un-American. *The Federalist*, May 2.

Fisher, J. D., and Johnson, D. S. (2020). Inequality and mobility over the past half century using income, consumption and wealth. https://www.nber.org/system/files/chapters/c14444/c14444.pdf

Fleurbaey, M. (2007). Poverty as a form of oppression. In T. Pogge (ed.), *Freedom from Poverty as a Human Right: Who Owes What to the Very Poor?* Oxford University Press, pp. 133–154.

Fordham, S., and Ogbu, J. U. (1986). Black students' school success: Coping with the "burden of 'acting white.'" *The Urban Review*, 18(3), 176–206. https://doi.org/10.1007/BF01112192

Franklin, J. H., and Moss, A. A. J. (2000). *From Slavery to Freedom: A History of African Americans.* Alfred A. Knopf.

Free, L. (2015). *Suffrage Reconstructed: Gender, Race, and Voting Rights in the Civil War Era.* Cornell University Press.

Gendadek, K., and West, K. (2011). Family friendly wage occupations and wage differentials. Population Association of America. https://pop.umn.edu/sites/pop.umn.edu/files/family-friendly_occupations.pdf

Gibson, M. A., and Ogbu, J. U. (1991). *Minority Status and Schooling: A Comparative Study of Immigrant and Involuntary Minorities.* Garland Publishing.

Gilbert, S. (2017). The movement of #MeToo. *The Atlantic*, October 16.

# References

Girnus, A. C. (2021,). Las Vegas charter school sued for curriculum covering race, identity. *Nevada Current*, January 21.

Goldberg, Z. (2019). Threadreader. Twitter. https://threadreaderapp.com/thread/1133828459917193218.html

Goldin, C. (1990). *Understanding the Gender Gap: An Economic History of American Women*. Oxford University Press.

Goldin, C. (2006). The quiet revolution that transformed women's employment, education, and family. *American Economic Review*, 96(2), 1–21. https://doi.org/10.1257/00 0282806777212350

Gonzales, S. (2021). Gonzales: Biden's immigration action reflects vision of our nation as one that welcomes immigrants. Center on Budget and Policy Priorities. https://www .cbpp.org/press/statements/gonzales-bidens-immigration-action-reflects-vision-of-our-nation-as-one-that

Gordon, C. (2014). A tattered safety net: Social policy and American inequality. *Dissent*, April 3.

Graham, J., Haidt, J., and Nosek, B. A. (2009). Liberals and conservatives rely on different sets of moral foundations. *Journal of Personality and Social Psychology*, 96(5), 1029–1046. https://doi.org/10.1037/a0015141

Gramm, P., and Early, J. (2021). Incredible shrinking income inequality. *Wall Street Journal*, March 23. https://www.wsj .com/articles/incredible-shrinking-income-inequality-1161 6517284

Greene, J. (2013). *Moral Tribes: Emotion, Reason, and the Gap Between Us and Them*. Penguin.

Haidt, J. (2001). The emotional dog and its rational tail: A social intuitionist approach to moral judgment. *Psychological Review*, 108(4), 814–834. https://doi.org/10 .1037/0033-295X.108.4.814

Haidt, J. (2012). *The Righteous Mind: Why Good People Are Divided by Politics and Religion*. Pantheon.

Haidt, J., and Lukianoff, G. (2018). *The Coddling of the*

# References

*American Mind: How Good Intentions and Bad Ideas Are Setting Up a Generation for Failure.* Penguin.

Hardeman, R. R., Medina, E. M., and Kozhimannil, K. B. (2016). Structural racism and supporting black lives – the role of health professionals. *New England Journal of Medicine, 375,* 2113–2115.

Harding, S. (1981). Family reform movements: Recent feminism and its opposition. *Feminist Studies, 7*(1), 57–75.

Hassell, H., Holbein, J., and Miles, M. (2020). Journalists may be liberal, but this doesn't affect which candidates they choose to cover. *The Washington Post,* April 10.

Hedges, S. (2020). Diversity, equity, and inclusion in K-12 professional development: The mission versus the reality. *Heterdox Academy: The Blog.* https://heterodoxacademy .org/blog/diversity-equity-and-inclusion-in-k-12-profession al-development-the-mission-versus-the-reality

Hellmer, R. (2013). Affirmative action is fair, necessary to make up for opportunities lost to minorities. *Kansas State: The Collegian,* April 22.

Helo, A., and Onuf, P. (2003). Jefferson, morality, and the problem of slavery. *The William and Mary Quarterly, 60*(3), 583–614.

Henderson, D. R. (2018). Income inequality isn't the problem. Hoover Institution. https://www.hoover.org/research /income-inequality-isnt-problem

Hill, E., Tiefenthaler, A., Triebert, C., Jordan, D., Willis, H., and Stein, R. (2020). How George Floyd was killed in police custody. *The New York Times,* May 31. https:// www.nytimes.com/2020/05/31/us/george-floyd-investiga tion.html

Hinrichs, P. (2012). The effects of affirmative action bans on college enrollment, educational attainment, and the demographic composition at universities. *The Review of Economics and Statistics, 94*(3), 712–722.

Holzer, H. J., and Neumark, D. (2000). What does

affirmative action do? *Industrial and Labor Relations Review*, 53(2), 240–271. https://doi.org/10.1177/00197939 0005300204

Holzer, H. J., and Neumark, D. (2006). Affirmative action: What do we know? *Journal of Policy Analysis and Management*, 25(2), 463–490.

Horowitz, J. M., Brown, A., and Cox, K. (2019). Race in America 2019. Pew Research Center, April 9. https://www .pewresearch.org/social-trends/2019/04/09/race-in-america -2019

Horowitz, J. M., Igielnik, R., and Kochhar, R. (2020). Most Americans say there is too much economic inequality in the U.S., but fewer than half call it a top priority. Pew Research Center, January 9. https://www.pewresearch.org/social-trends/2020/01/09/most-americans-say-there-is-too-much -economic-inequality-in-the-u-s-but-fewer-than-half-call-it -a-top-priority

Horwitz, S. (2017). The unfairness of equal outcomes. Foundation for Economic Education, April 28. https://fee .org/articles/the-unfairness-of-equal-outcomes

Hsin, A., and Xie, Y. (2014). Explaining Asian Americans' academic advantage over whites. *Proceedings of the National Academy of Sciences of the United States of America*, 111(23), 8416–8421. https://doi.org/10.1073/pn as.1406402111

Hughes, C. (2018). The racism treadmill. *Quillette*, May 14. https://quillette.com/2018/05/14/the-racism-treadmill

Hughes, C. (2020). A better anti-racism. *Persuasion*, August 19. https://www.persuasion.community/p/a-better-anti-ra cism

Husock, H. (2008). Bring back assimilation. *City Journal*, May 13.

Iceland, J. (2013). *Poverty in America: A Handbook*, 3rd edition. University of California Press.

Iceland, J. (2017). *Race and Ethnicity in America*. University of California Press.

# References

Iceland, J., and Redstone, I. (2020). The declining earnings gap between young women and men in the United States, 1979–2018. *Social Science Research*, published online September 28. https://doi.org/10.1016/j.ssresearch.2020.102479

Iceland, J., and Sharp, G. (2013). White residential segregation in U.S. metropolitan areas: Conceptual issues, patterns, and trends from the U.S. census, 1980 to 2010. *Population Research and Policy Review*, 32(5), 663–686. https://doi.org/10.1007/s11113-013-9277-6

International Rescue Committee (2021). Why should America take in more refugees? Get the facts on the refugee cap. https://www.rescue.org/article/why-should-america-take-more-refugees-get-facts-refugee-cap

Iyengar, S., Lelkes, Y., Levendusky, M., Malhotra, N., and Westwood, S. J. (2019). The origins and consequences of affective polarization in the United States. *Annual Review of Political Science*, 22, 129–146. https://doi.org/10.1146/annurev-polisci-051117-073034

Johnson, P., and Vega, M. (2019). Strategies for increasing girls' participation in STEM. Intercultural Development Research Association, October. https://www.idra.org/resource-center/strategies-for-increasing-girls-participation-in-stem

Juhn, C., and McCue, K. (2017). Specialization then and now: Marriage, children, and the gender earnings gap across cohorts. *Journal of Economic Perspectives*, 31(1), 183–204. https://doi.org/10.1257/jep.31.1.183

Justman, M., and Stiassnie, H. (2021). Intergenerational mobility in lifetime income. *Review of Income and Wealth*, 67(4), 928–949. https://doi.org/10.1111/roiw.12505

Kasinitz, P., Mollenkopf, J. H., Waters, M. C., and Holdaway, J. (2008). *Inheriting the City: The Children of Immigrants Come of Age*. Harvard University Press.

Kendi, I. X. (2019a). *How to Be an Antiracist*. One World.

Kendi, I. X. (2019b). Pass an anti-racist constitutional

amendment. *Politico*. https://www.politico.com/interactives
/2019/how-to-fix-politics-in-america/inequality/pass-an-anti-
racist-constitutional-amendment

Kinser, A. (2004). Negotiating spaces for/through third-wave
feminism. *NWSA Journal, 16*(3), 124–153.

Kling, A. (2017). *The Three Languages of Politics*. Cato
Institute.

Kukathas, C. (2004). The case for open immigration. In
C. Wellman and A. Cohen (eds.), *Contemporary Debates
in Applied Ethics*. Wiley-Blackwell, pp. 376–390.

Kuypers, J. A. (2014). *Partisan Jounalism: A History of Media
Bias in the United States*. Rowman & Littlefield.

Larrimore, J., Burkhauser, R. V., Auten, G., and Armour, P.
(2021). Recent trends in US income distributions in tax
record data using more comprehensive measures of income
including real accrued capital gains. *Journal of Political
Economy, 129*(5), 1319–1360. https://doi.org/10.1086/71
3098

Leaper, C., and Friedman, C. K. (2007). The socializa-
tion of gender. In J. E. Grusec and P. D. Hastings (eds.),
*Handbook of Socialisation: Theory and Research*. Guilford
Publications, pp. 561–587.

Leef, G. (2022). The unseen costs of Covid mania. *The
National Review*, January 1. https://www.nationalreview
.com/corner/the-unseen-costs-of-covid-mania

Lewis, T. (2021). How the U.S. pandemic response went
wrong – and what went right – during a year of COVID.
*Scientific American*, March 11. https://www.scientificamer
ican.com/article/how-the-u-s-pandemic-response-went-wr
ong-and-what-went-right-during-a-year-of-covid

Lippa, R. A. (2010). Gender differences in personality and
interests: When, where, and why? *Social and Personality
Psychology Compass, 4*(11), 1098–1110. https://doi.org
/10.1111/j.1751-9004.2010.00320.x

Lodge, H. C. (1891). The restriction of immigration. *The
North American Review, 152*(410), 27–36.

# References

Lopez, M. H., Passel., J. S., and Cohn, D. (2021). Key facts about the changing U.S. unauthorized immigrant population. Pew Research Center, April 13. https://www.pew research.org/fact-tank/2021/04/13/key-facts-about-the-changing-u-s-unauthorized-immigrant-population

Loury, G. C. (2020). The bias narrative v. the development narrative. *City Journal*, December 8.

Mac Donald, H. (2018). *The Diversity Delusion: How Race and Gender Pandering Corrupt the University and Undermine Our Culture*. St. Martin's Press.

Mac Donald, H. (2020). Breakdown. *City Journal*, July 1.

McCall, L., and Percheski, C. (2010). Income inequality: New trends and research directions. *Annual Review of Sociology*, 36, 329–347. https://doi.org/10.1146/annurev .soc.012809.102541

McCammond, A. (2015). Brown University announces $100 million anti-Racism plan. *Cosmopolitan*, November 23. https://www.cosmopolitan.com/college/news/a49765/bro wn-university-announces-anti-racism-plan

McElwee, S. (2014). How Thomas Piketty and Elizabeth Warren demolished the conventional wisdom on debt. *Salon*, May 18. https://www.salon.com/2014/05/18/how _thomas_piketty_and_elizabeth_warren_demolished_the _conventional_wisdom_on_debt

McGreal, C. (2019). "You can't win": The parents working full-time – and stuggling to survive. *The Guardian*, April 30.

McIntosh, P. (2003). White privilege: Unpacking the invisible knapsack. In S. Plous (ed.), *Understanding Prejudice and Discrimination*. New York: McGraw-Hill, pp. 191–196.

McLanahan, S. (2004). Diverging destinies: How children are faring under the second demographic transition. *Demography*, 41(4), 607–627.

MacLaury, J. (2010). President Kennedy's E.O. 10925: Seedbed of affirmative action. *Federal History*, 2(2), 42–57.

# References

MacPherson, L. (2007). The value of multiculturalism. *Toronto Star*, January 1.

Maddeaux, S. (2021). Lockdowns are killing young Canadians. *National Post*, December 30. https://national post.com/opinion/sabrina-maddeaux-lockdowns-are-kil ling-young-canadians

Mann, A., and DiPrete, T. A. (2013). Trends in gender segregation in the choice of science and engineering majors. *Social Science Research*, 42(6), 1519–1541. https://doi.org /10.1016/j.ssresearch.2013.07.002

Marietta, M., and Barker, D. C. (2019). *One Nation, Two Realities: Dueling Fact Perceptions in American Society*. Oxford University Press.

Martin, J. A., Hamilton, B. E., Osterman, M. J. K., Driscoll, A. K., and Drake, P. (2018). Births: final for 2017. *National Vital Statistics Reports*, 67(8), 1–49. https://www.cdc.gov /nchs/data_access/Vitalstatsonline.htm

Martin, P., and Midgley, E. (2003). *Immigration: Shaping and Reshaping America. Population Bulletin*, 58(2). https:// www.prb.org/resources/population-bulletin-vol-58-no-2- immigration-shaping-and-reshaping-america

Massey, D. S., Charles, C. Z., Lundy, G. F., and Fischer, M. J. (2003). *The Source of the River: The Social Origins of Freshmen at America's Selective Colleges and Universities*. Princeton University Press.

Massey, D. S., and Denton, N. (1993). *American Apartheid: Segregation and the Making of the Underclass*. Harvard University Press.

Mendes, K. (2011). Framing feminism: News coverage of the women's movement in British and American newspapers, 1968–1982. *Social Movement Studies*, 10(1), 81–98. https://doi.org/10.1080/14742837.2011.545228

Meyer, B. D., Wu, D., Mooers, V., and Medalia, C. (2021). The use and misuse of income data and extreme poverty in the United States. *Journal of Labor Economics*, 39(S1), S5–S58. https://doi.org/10.1086/711227

# References

Migration Policy Institute (2021). Top 25 destinations of international migrants. https://www.migrationpolicy.org /programs/data-hub/charts/top-25-destinations-internatio nal-migrants

Miller, C. C., Badger, E., Hurd, N., Kendi, I. X., Hendren, N., and Chetty, R. (2018). "When I see racial disparities, I see racism." Discussing race, gender and mobility. *The New York Times*. https://www.nytimes.com/interactive/2018/03 /27/upshot/reader-questions-about-race-gender-and-mobil ity.html

Mills, N. (1994). *Debating Affirmative Action: Race, Gender, Ethnicity, and the Politics of Inclusion*. Delta.

Minkel, J. (2018). How to teach boys to be better men. *Education Week*, October 1.

Molla, R. (2020). Social media is making a bad political situation worse. Vox, November 10. https://www.vox.com/re code/21534345/polarization-election-social-media-filter- bubble

Mooney, M., Charles, C. Z., and Torres, K. (2007). Black immigrants and black natives attending selective colleges and universities in the United States. *American Journal of Education*, 113(2), 243–271.

Mortensen, R. W. (2012). *Understanding Illegal Aliens and Illegal Immigration*. Center for Immigration Studies, April 25. https://cis.org/Mortensen/Understanding-Illegal-Aliens -and-Illegal-Immigration

Moynihan, D. P. (1965). *The Negro Family: The Case for National Action*. US Department of Labor.

Moynihan, D. P. (1983). More than social security was at stake. *The Washington Post*, January 18.

Mulvaney, E. (2020). Diversity-fueled "reverse" bias claims put employers in quandary. *Bloomberg Law*, October 8. https://www.bloomberglaw.com/bloomberglawnews/daily -labor-report/X4SEPJ98000000?bna_news_filter=daily-labor -report#jcite

# References

Murray, C. A. (2012). *Coming Apart: The State of White America, 1960–2010*. Crown Forum.

National Academies (2017). *The Economic and Fiscal Consequences of Immigration*. The National Academies Press.

National Public Radio (2014). Phyllis Schlafly explains why feminism has made women unhappy. July 21. https://www.npr.org/2014/07/21/333582322/phyllis-schlafly-explains-why-feminism-has-made-women-unhappy

Newman, E. (2021). 10 reasons to wear a mask. *The Humanist*, September 16. https://thehumanist.com/commentary/10-reasons-to-wear-a-mask

OECD (2021). Poverty rate. OECD Data. https://data.oecd.org/inequality/poverty-rate.htm

Ogbu, J. U. (1978). *Minority Education and Caste: The American System in Cross-Cultural Perspective*. Academic Press.

Ogbu, J. U. (1991). Minority coping responses and school experience – ProQuest. *The Journal of Psychohistory*, *18*(4), 433–456. https://search.proquest.com/docview/1305586802?pq-origsite=gscholar

Ogbu, J. U. (2003). *No Black American Students in an Affluent Suburb: A Study of Academic Disengagement*. Lawrence Erlbaum.

Otteson, J. R. (2011). The unintended consequences of the welfare state. *Forbes*, April 25. https://www.forbes.com/2011/04/25/welfare-labor-immoral.html?sh=76e628593867

Ousey, G. C., and Kubrin, C. E. (2018). Immigration and crime: Assessing a contentious issue. *Annual Review of Criminology*, *1*, 63–84.

Oxfam (2022). Inequality kills. https://oxfamilibrary.openrepository.com/bitstream/handle/10546/621341/bp-inequality-kills-170122-en.pdf

Pager, D., Western, B., and Bonikowski, B. (2009). Discrimination in a low-wage labor market: A field experiment. *American Sociological Review*, 74(5), 777–799. https://doi.org/10.1177/000312240907400505

Parvini, N. (2018). Why assumptions about "rising inequality" are wrong. *Quillette*, October 4. https://quillette.com /2018/10/04/why-assumptions-about-rising-inequality-are -wrong

Patterson, J. T. (2000). *America's Struggle Against Poverty in the 21st Century*. Harvard University Press.

Pendergast, P. M., Wadsworth, T., and LePree, J. (2018). Immigration, crime, and victimization in the US context: An overview. In R. Martinez Jr., M. Hollis, and J. I. Stowell (eds.), *The Handbook of Race, Ethnicity, Crime, and Justice*. John Wiley & Sons, pp. 65–85.

Perlmann, J. (2005). *Italians Then, Mexicans Now: Immigrant Origins and Second-Generation Progress, 1980 to 2000*. Russell Sage Foundation.

Perry, M. J. (2017). There really is no "gender wage gap." There's a "gender earnings gap" but "paying women well" won't close that gap. American Enterprise Institute, July 31. https://www.aei.org/carpe-diem/there-really-is-no-gen der-wage-gap-there-is-a-gender-earnings-gap-but-paying -women-well-wont-close-that-gap

Perry, M. J. (2018). Table of the Day: Bachelor's degrees for the Class of 2016 by field and gender. Oh, and the overall 25.6% degree gap for men! American Enterprise Institute, June 19. https://www.aei.org/carpe-diem/table-of-the-day -masters-degrees-for-the-class-of-2016-by-field-and-gender -oh-and-the-overall-31-masters-degree-gap-for-men

Perry, M. J., and Biggs, A. G. (2018). Equal Pay Day celebrates a tiresome myth that just won't die. American Enterprise Institute, April 10. https://www.aei.org/articles/equal-pay -day-celebrates-a-tiresome-myth-that-just-wont-die

Pew Research Center (2010). The decline of marriage and the rise of new families. https://doi.org/10.4324/9781315081 373-3

# References

Pew Research Center (2021a). Most Americans are critical of government's handling of situation at US.-mexico border. https://www.pewresearch.org/politics/2021/05/03/most -americans-are-critical-of-governments-handling-of-situa tion-at-u-s-mexico-border

Pew Research Center (2021b). Political typology: Beyond red vs. blue. https://www.pewresearch.org/politics/2021/11/09 /beyond-red-vs-blue-the-political-typology-2

Pfankuch, B. (2019). Thousands of kids struggle with poverty in South Dakota. *Rapid City Journal*, February 10.

Pinker, S. (2016). *The Blank Slate: The Modern Denial of Human Nature*. Penguin.

Portes, A., and Rumbaut, R. G. (2001). *Legacies: The Stories of the Immigrant Second Generation*. University of California Press.

Poujoulat, A.-C. (2020). Protests across the globe after George Floyd's death. *CNN*, June 13.

Putnam, R. D. (2007). *E Pluribus Unum:* Diversity and community in the twenty-first century: The 2006 Johan Skytte Prize Lecture, *Scandinavian Political Studies*, 30(2), 137–174.

Quillian, L., Pager, D., Hexel, O., and Midtbøen, A. H. (2017). Meta-analysis of field experiments shows no change in racial discrimination in hiring over time. *Proceedings of the National Academy of Sciences of the United States of America, 114*(41), 10870–10875. https://doi.org/10.1073 /pnas.1706255114

Rauch, J. (2021). *The Constitution of Knowledge: A Defense of Truth*. The Brookings Institution.

Rector, R. (2014). How welfare undermines marriage and what to do about it. http://thf_media.s3.amazonaws.com /2014/pdf/IB4302.pdf

*Regents of the University of California v. Bakke*, 438 U.S. 265 (1978).

Reich, R. (2016). Robert Reich: The economy is rigged against ordinary people. *Newsweek*, September 6. https://www.

newsweek.com/robert-reich-economy-rigged-against-ordi
nary-people-495931

Reskin, B. (1998). *The Realities of Affirmative Action in Employment*. American Sociological Association.

Reynolds, R. (2021). Court rules against using race, sex to allocate federal aid. *Associated Press*, May 28. https://www
.usnews.com/news/us/articles/2021-05-28/court-rules-against
-using-race-sex-to-allocate-federal-aid

Riley, J. (2014). *Please Stop Helping Us: How Liberals Make It Harder for Blacks to Succeed*. Encounter Books.

Ross, S. L., and Turner, M. A. (2005). Housing discrimina-
tion in metropolitan America: Explaining changes between 1989 and 2000. *Social Problems*, 52(2), 152–180. https://
doi.org/10.1525/sp.2005.52.2.152

Routledge, C., and Schwarz, G. (2021). UBI is not a recipe for long-term human flourishing. *Newsweek*, March 22.

Rowe, I. (2020). The power of personal agency. *The Wall Street Journal*, June 21.

Ruiz-Grossman, S. (2021). DACA recipients were "candid" with Biden about "high stakes" of immigration reform. *HuffPost*, May 14. https://www.huffpost.com/entry/joe-bi
den-dreamers-daca-white-house-immigration_n_609efdd0
e4b03e1dd389d698

Saez, E., and Zucman, G. (2020). The rise of income and wealth inequality in America: Evidence from distribu-
tional macroeconomic accounts. *Journal of Economic Perspectives*, 34(4), 3–26. https://doi.org/10.1257/JEP.34
.4.3

Sakamoto, A., Amaral, E. F. L., Wang, S. X., and Nelson, C. (2021). The socioeconomic attainments of second-
generation Nigerian and other Black Americans: Evidence from the current population survey, 2009 to 2019. *Socius*, 7. https://doi.org/10.1177/23780231211001971

Sakamoto, A., Goyette, K., and Kim, C. (2009). Socioeconomic attainments of Asian Americans. *Annual Review of Sociology*, 35, 255–276.

# References

Sampson, R. J. (2008). Rethinking crime and immigration. *Contexts* (Winter), 28–33. https://doi.org/10.1525/ctx.20 08.7.1.28.winter

Scarborough, W. J., Sin, R., and Risman, B. (2019). Attitudes and the stalled gender revolution: Egalitarianism, traditionalism, and ambivalence from 1977 through 2016. *Gender and Society*, *33*(2), 173–200. https://doi.org/10.1177/0891 243218809604

Schleeter, R. (2013). Teaching tolerance. National Geographic. https://media.nationalgeographic.org/assets/reference/asse ts/teaching-tolerance-1.pdf

Scott, D. (2020). Flattening the curve worked – until it didn't. *Vox*, December 31. https://www.vox.com/22180261/covid -19-coronavirus-social-distancing-lockdowns-flatten-the -curve

Semega, J., Kollar, M., Shrider, E. A., and Creamer, J. F. (2020). Income and poverty in the United States: 2019. US Census Bureau, September, https://www.census.gov/conte nt/dam/Census/library/publications/2020/demo/p60-270 .pdf

Sen, A. (1999). *Development as Freedom*. Anchor Books.

Sharkey, P. (2016). Neighborhoods, cities, and economic mobility. *The Russell Sage Foundation Journal of the Social Sciences*, *2*(2), 159–177. https://doi.org/10.4324/97 80429499821-38

Shemla, M., and Post, C. (2015). The dark side of Silicon Valley diversity targets. *Newsweek*, September 19.

Shrider, E. A., Kollar, M., Chen, F., and Semega, J. (2021). Income and poverty in the United States: 2020. US Census Bureau, September, https://www.census.gov/content/dam /Census/library/publications/2021/demo/p60-273.pdf

Silver, E., Goff, K., and Iceland, J. (2022). Social order and social justice: Moral intuitions, systemic racism beliefs, and Americans' divergent attitudes toward Black Lives Matter and police. *Criminology*, *60*(2), 342–369. https://doi.org /10.1111/1745-9125.12303

# References

Silver, E., and Silver, S. (2021). The influence of moral intuitions on Americans' divergent reactions to reports of sexual assault and harassment. *Journal of Interpersonal Violence*, published online October 15. https://doi.org/10.1177/0886 2605211050102

Smith, A., Hughes, A., Remy, E., and Shah, S. (2020). Democrats on Twitter more liberal, less focused on compromise than those not on the platform. Pew Research Center, February 3. https://www.pewresearch.org/fact-tank /2020/02/03/democrats-on-twitter-more-liberal-less-focused-on-compromise-than-those-not-on-the-platform

Smith, C. (2014). *The Sacred Project of American Sociology*. Oxford University Press.

Solon, G. (2017). Intergenerational transmission of income inequality: What do we know? *Focus*, *33*(2), 3–5.

Sowell, T. (2005). *Black Rednecks and White Liberals*. Encounter Books.

Sowell, T. (2007). *A Conflict of Visions: Ideological Origins of Political Struggles*. Basic Books.

Sowell, T. (2011). Defining "poverty" to benefit the welfare state. *The New American*, August 3.

Stark, S. (2004). Taking responsibility for oppression: Affirmative action and racial injustice. *Public Affairs Quarterly*, *18*(3), 205–221.

Stoet, G., and Geary, D. C. (2018). The gender-equality paradox in science, technology, engineering, and mathematics education. *Psychological Science*, *29*(4), 581–593. https:// doi.org/10.1177/0956797617741719

Styrna, P. (2021). 5 reasons why amnesty is a bad idea. Federation for American Immigration Reform (FAIR). February. https://www.fairus.org/issue/amnesty/5-reasons -why-amnesty-bad-idea

Sullivan, A. (2018). It's time to resist the excesses of #MeToo. *New York Magazine*, January 12. https://nymag.com/intell igencer/2018/01/andrew-sullivan-time-to-resist-excesses-of -metoo.html

# References

Teaching Tolerance (2016). Social justice standards: The teaching tolerance anti-bias framework. https://www.learningforjustice.org/sites/default/files/2017-06/TT_Social_Justice_Standards_0.pdf

Telles, E. E., and Ortiz, V. (2008). *Generations of Exclusion: Mexican Americans, Assimilation, and Race*. Russell Sage Foundation.

Tello, M. (2017). Racism and discrimination in health care: Providers and patients. *Harvard Health Blog*, January 16. https://www.health.harvard.edu/blog/racism-discrimination-health-care-providers-patients-2017011611015

Terborg, J. R., Peters, L. H., Ilgen, D. R., and Smith, F. (1977). Organizational and personal correlates of attitudes toward women as managers. *Academy of Management Journal*, 20(1), 89–100. https://doi.org/10.5465/255464

The Heritage Foundation (2021). What immigration reform should look like. https://www.heritage.org/immigration/heritage-explains/what-immigration-reform-should-look

The New York Times (1965). Immigration impasse (June 18).

Torche, F. (2015). Analyses of intergenerational mobility: An interdisciplinary review. *Annals of the American Academy of Political and Social Science*, 657(1), 37–62. https://doi.org/10.1177/0002716214547476

Turner, J. H. (2019). The more American sociology seeks to become a politically-relevant discipline, the more irrelevant it becomes to solving societal problems. *American Sociologist*, 50(4), 456–487. https://doi.org/10.1007/s12108-019-09420-5

Turner, J. H., Beeghley, L., and Powers, C. H. (2012). *The Emergence of Sociological Theory*, 7th edition. Sage.

Turner, M. A., and Skidmore, F. (1999). *Mortgage Lending Discrimination: A Review of Existing Evidence*. Urban Institute Press.

Tyko, K. (2020). These cleaners kill coronavirus: Lysol, Clorox, Purell products make EPA's disinfectants list. *USA Today*. https://www.usatoday.com/story/money/2020/03/0

5/prepare-for-coronavirus-epa-disinfectants-list-covid-19
/4966691002

UC San Diego (2021). Contributions to diversity statements. Center for Faculty Diversity and Inclusion. https://faculty diversity.ucsd.edu/recruitment/contributions-to-diversity .html

University of Southern California (2020). How to be anti-racist: A social worker's perspective. USC Suzanne Dworak-Peck School of Social Work. https://msw.usc.edu/mswusc -blog/how-to-be-antiracist

Urofsky, M. I. (2020). *The Affirmative Action Puzzle: A Living History from Reconstruction to Today*. Pantheon Books.

US Bureau of Labor Statistics (2012). *Women in the Labor Force: A Databook*. https://www.bls.gov/opub/reports/wo mens-databook/archive/womenlaborforce_2012.pdf

US Bureau of Labor Statistics (2017). *Women in the Labor Force: A Databook*. https://www.bls.gov/opub/reports/wo mens-databook/2017/home.htm

US Bureau of Labor Statistics (2021). Table 3.3. Civilian labor force participation rate by age, sex, race, and ethnicity. https://www.bls.gov/emp/tables/civilian-labor-force-partici pation-rate.htm

US Census Bureau (2019). Table P-38. Full-time, year-round workers by median earnings and sex: 1960 to 2018. Historical Income Tables: People. https://www.census.gov /data/tables/time-series/demo/income-poverty/historical-in come-people.html

US Census Bureau (2020a). Table 2. Poverty status of people by family relationship, race, and Hispanic origin. Historical Poverty Tables: People and Families, 1959 to 2020. https:// www.census.gov/data/tables/time-series/demo/income -poverty/historical-poverty-people.html

US Census Bureau (2020b). Table A-2. Percent of people 25 years and over who have completed high school or college, by race, Hispanic origin and sex: Selected years, 1940 to

References

2020. Historical Time Series Tables. https://www.census
.gov/data/tables/time-series/demo/educational-attainment
/cps-historical-time-series.html

US Census Bureau (2020c). Table H-1. Income limits for each
fifth and top 5 percent of all households: 1967 to 2020.
Historical Income Tables: Households. https://www.census
.gov/data/tables/time-series/demo/income-poverty/historic
al-income-households.html

US Census Bureau (2020d). Table H-4. Gini ratios for
households, by race and Hispanic origin of householder.
Historical Income Tables: Households. https://www.census
.gov/data/tables/time-series/demo/income-poverty/historic
al-income-households.html

US Census Bureau (2020e). Table H-5. Race and Hispanic
origin of householder – households by median and mean
income. Historical Income Tables: Households. https://
www.census.gov/data/tables/time-series/demo/income
-poverty/historical-income-households.html

US Census Bureau (2020f). Table P-40. Women's earnings as
a percentage of men's earnings by race and Hispanic origin:
1960 to 2020. Historical Income Tables: People. https://
www.census.gov/data/tables/time-series/demo/income-pov
erty/historical-income-people.html

US Census Bureau (2021a). Table 4. Poverty status of families,
by type of family, presence of related children, race, and
Hispanic origin: 1959 to 2020. Historical Poverty Tables:
People and Families, 1959 to 2020. https://www.census
.gov/data/tables/time-series/demo/income-poverty/historic
al-poverty-people.html

US Census Bureau (2021b). Table B05003D. Sex by age by
nativity and citizenship status (Asian alone). Data.Cen
sus.Gov, American Community Survey 1-Year Estimates
Detailed Tables. https://www.census.gov/topics/population
/foreign-born/guidance/acs-guidance/acs-by-subject.html

US Census Bureau (2021c). Table B05003I. Sex by age by
nativity and citizenship status (Hispanic or Latino). Da

# References

ta.Census.Gov, American Community Survey 1-Year Estimates Detailed Tables. https://www.census.gov/topics /population/foreign-born/guidance/acs-guidance/acs-by -subject.html

US Department of Homeland Security (2022). Table 2. Persons obtaining permanent resident status: Fiscal years 1820 to 2020. *Yearbook of Immigration Statistics*. https:// www.dhs.gov/immigration-statistics/yearbook/2018/table2

US Department of Labor (2009). *An Analysis of Reasons for the Disparity in Wages Between Men and Women*. https:// www.shrm.org/hr-today/public-policy/hr-public-policy-issues /documents/gender%20wage%20gap%20final%20report .pdf

US Department of Labor (2020). *Labor Force Participation Rates*. https://www.dol.gov/agencies/wb/data/latest-annual -data/labor-force-participation-rates

US Department of State (2022). Policy Issues. Refugee and humanitarian assistance. https://www.state.gov/policy-issu es/refugee-and-humanitarian-assistance

Vallicella, W. F. (2021). What is wrong with illegal immigration? https://williamfvallicella.substack.com/p/what-is-wrong-with-illegal-immigration

VanDusky-Allen, J., and Shvetsova, O. (2021). How America's partisan divide over pandemic responses played out in the states. *The Conversation*, May 12. https://theconversation .com/how-americas-partisan-divide-over-pandemic-respon ses-played-out-in-the-states-157565

Vary, A. B. (2021). Oscars nominate most diverse acting slate ever, including first Asian American Best Actor. *Variety*, March 15.

Velasquez, D., Kondo, J., Downer, S., and Broad Leib, E. (2020). Maximizing food security for unauthorized immigrants during COVID-19. *Health Affairs*, July 28. https:// www.healthaffairs.org/do/10.1377/hblog20200724.40740 /full

von Spakovsky, H. A. (2018). Don't believe the myths about

# References

Dreamers. The Heritage Foundation, January 16. https://
www.heritage.org/immigration/commentary/dont-believe
-the-myths-about-dreamers

Vosoughi, S., Roy, D., and Aral, S. (2018). The spread of true
and false news online. *Science*, *359*(6380), 1146–1151.
https://news.1242.com/article/148290

Wagmiller Jr., R. L., and Adelman, R. M. (2009). Childhood
and intergenerational poverty. National Center for Children
in Poverty. http://academiccommons.columbia.edu/catalog
/ac:126233

Wang, S. X., Takei, I., and Sakamoto, A. (2017). Do Asian
Americans face labor market discrimination? Accounting
for the cost of living among native-born men and women.
*Socius*, *3*, 1–14. https://doi.org/10.1177/237802311774
1724

Wang, W., and Wilcox, W. B. (2018). *The Millennial Success
Sequence: Marriage, Kids, and the "Success Sequence"
among Young Adults*. Institute for Family Studies. https://
aei.org/wp-content/uploads/2017/06/IFS-MillennialSuccess
Sequence-Final.pdf

Ward, S. F. (2016). Women outnumber men in law schools
for first time, newly updated data show. *ABA Journal*,
December 19.

Wellons, T. (2019). Affirmative action is still an effective and
necessary tool. *Contexts*, *18*(1), 80.

Wilson, W. J. (1987). *The Truly Disadvantaged: The Inner
City, the Underclass, and Public Policy*. University of
Chicago Press.

Yang, A. (2019). Yang2020. https://2020.yang2020.com/po
licies/the-freedom-dividend

Zarya, V. (2018). The share of female CEOs in the Fortune
500 dropped by 25% in 2018. *Fortune*, May 21.

# Index

# Index

# Index

# Index

# Index

# Index

# Index

# Index

wage(s) *(cont.)*
  non-wage benefits, 53
  transparency, 42
war, 132
  Civil War, 71
  Syrian civil war, 137–8
  World War II, 134, 136
wealth, 39, 85, 110, 113, 116,
    120, 126–7, 129
Weinstein, Harvey, 3
welfare,
  of the individual / group, *see*
    morality
  programs, 64–5, 115, 124–5,
    127, 136–40, 150–1
  state, 125–9

Wellons, Tonia, 107
White Privilege, 69, 71, 83–5
white supremacy, 71–2, 78
Whiteness, 69
whites
  culture, 96, 149
  discrimination against, 78,
    98, 103, 133
  family structure, 88–9
  immigration, 133–5
  socioeconomic status, 71–6,
    91–4, 105
women's movement, *see*
  feminism

Yang, Andrew, 127–8